THE ENGLISH
CATHEDRAL

THE ENGLISH CATHEDRAL

Text by
TIM TATTON-BROWN

Photography by
JOHN CROOK

NEW HOLLAND

First published in 2002 by New Holland Publishers (UK) Ltd
London • Cape Town • Sydney • Auckland

10 9 8 7 6 5 4 3 2 1

www.newhollandpublishers.com

Garfield House, 86–88 Edgware Road, London W2 2EA,
United Kingdom

80 McKenzie Street, Cape Town 8001, South Africa

14 Aquatic Drive, Frenchs Forest, NSW 2086, Australia

218 Lake Road, Northcote, Auckland, New Zealand

ISBN 1 84330 120 2

Publishing Manager: Jo Hemmings
Senior Editor: Kate Michell
Editor: Charlotte Rundall
Editorial Assistant: Anne Konopelski
Designer & Cover Design: Alan Marshall
Production: Joan Woodroffe
Cartography: William Smuts
Index: Dorothy Frame

Reproduction by Pica Digital (Pte) Ltd, Singapore
Printed and bound in Singapore by Kyodo Printing Co.
(Singapore) Pte Ltd

PRELIMINARY PAGES

HALF-TITLE PAGE: A modern altar and candles mark the site of the
shrine of St Richard in Chichester Cathedral.

TITLE PAGE: The view north across the lesser transept at Salisbury
Cathedral.

RIGHT: Derby Cathedral is full of early 18th- and 20th-century
Baroque splendours. This magnificent wrought-iron screen was made
by Robert Bakewell (1682–1752), a local smith whose work can be
found all over the Midlands.

PAGE 6: *left:* The view east up the nave of St Alban's Abbey;
right: A boss from Bishop Fox's presbytery vault at Winchester Cathedral,
depicting the Pelican in her Piety.

PAGE 7: *left:* A boss from Exter Cathedral depicting the head of a
14th-century king; *right:* View east through the choir and Trinity
chapel of Canterbury Cathedral.

AUTHOR'S ACKNOWLEDGEMENTS

The author, Tim Tatton-Brown, would like to thank his wife, Veronica,
for greatly helping with the word-processing of the manuscript, and
Kate Michell and all at New Holland Publishers for all their help and
editorial advice.

For Miranda and Lucy

CONTENTS

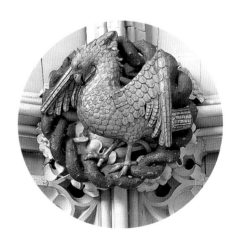

FOREWORD

IT IS AN ENORMOUS PRIVILEGE to have been invited to write the Foreword to this beautiful book. *The English Cathedral* traces the architectural, religious and spiritual histories of the cathedrals of England and, in doing so, draws attention not only to the role of cathedrals in the past but makes clear that they continue to be places of rich encounter, committed, each in their own way, to serving the needs of the communities in which they are set.

Those communities are increasing in their diversity and, as the years unfold, it is likely that English cathedrals will grow in importance as spaces for spiritual reflection, as well as continuing their daily duty as a place of worship. They will be places, too, where the very nature of faith and truth and the diversity of religious experience can be explored with openness of mind and generosity of heart.

One of the pioneer organisations concerned with the recognition and honouring of religious diversity, and utterly committed to combating prejudice and intolerance, is The Council of Christians and Jews. It was founded in the darkest days of the Second World War and continues its work today, believing that the creation of a just and tolerant society is a matter of the most profound importance.

Cathedrals are beautiful because so often they consist of a variety of styles of architecture. For me, those styles, in the way they play with and enhance each other, enrich our understanding, not only of beauty but of ourselves as human beings. It is as places committed to diversity in unity and unity in diversity that English cathedrals will continue to be treasured, explored and loved. We are blessed in their existence.

RIGHT: Constructed in the 1480s, the magnificent high reredos behind the high altar at St Alban's Abbey is similar in style to that found in Winchester cathedral.

The Rt Revd Christopher Herbert
Bishop of St Alban's Abbey
Chairman of The Council of Christians and Jews

PHOTOGRAPHER'S PREFACE

Visiting and photographing all of England's cathedrals in one concentrated burst has proved a fascinating challenge. The majority of the photographs in this book were taken between March and November 2001, and therefore provide a more or less 'instantaneous' view of England's cathedral architecture at the opening of the new millennium. Cathedrals are continuously developing, and this book includes many features – and even one brand-new cathedral, Middlesbrough – that have probably not appeared before in a volume of this kind.

At many of the cathedrals photographed, conservation or even new building works were taking place; few medieval cathedrals do not have scaffolding somewhere on the building as the rolling programme of repairs continues. This is occasionally apparent in my photographs, though in some cases the choice of subject was determined by the need to avoid areas where works made photography impossible.

I avoided introducing any form of extra, artificial lighting: natural light was the preferred option, supplemented on occasion by the individual cathedral's own lighting system. My main purpose here was to show off the architecture and furnishings of the various cathedrals as they are seen by the visitor.

A few other technical details may be of interest. The majority of the architectural images were taken on Fujichrome Provia 100F colour transparency film, using a 5 x 4 inch plate camera, allowing control of perspective and selective focus. Smaller details were photographed in 6 x 7 cm format.

The images could not have been obtained without the generous cooperation of the deans, canons and clergy, cathedral administrators, vergers and lay staff, and voluntary helpers of the 63 cathedrals featured in this book. I am also particularly grateful to all the cathedral authorities for kindly waiving the facility fees, which they normally have a right to expect.

Few people have had the privilege of visiting, let alone photographing, all of England's cathedrals. I hope my images will encourage readers to see for themselves not only the well-known medieval cathedrals of England, but also those lesser-known churches, which also contain architecture and furnishings of considerable charm and interest.

LEFT: A Nativity scene detail from the Genesis initial in the 12th-century Winchester Bible.

John Crook

ABOVE: The superb bishop's throne in Exeter Cathedral was made in 1313–16 with oaks from the bishop's own estates at Chudleigh and Newton St Cyres.

BELOW: The lines of the walls of the excavated Anglo-Saxon cathedral at Winchester are marked out on the grass on the north side of the nave.

INTRODUCTION

Today there are just over 60 cathedrals in England that were either built between the late 11th and the late 15th centuries, or in the 19th and 20th centuries – the one famous exception being the new St Paul's that was built in the late 17th century. Of these, about a dozen that were built in the Middle Ages are, in my opinion, the finest buildings ever to be erected in England or, dare one suggest, in the British Isles. Only in France, and to a lesser extent in Germany, Italy and Spain, can one find comparable or finer buildings. Cathedrals such as Canterbury and York, Lincoln and Winchester or Durham and Salisbury are some of the greatest works of architecture ever to have been erected anywhere in the world, though it is hard to compare them with other uniquely splendid buildings, such as the pyramids in Egypt; the Parthenon in Athens; the Angkor Wat temples in South-East Asia; Hagia Sophia and the Süleymaniye Mosque in Istanbul; and the Taj Mahal at Agra.

This book attempts to look briefly at all 63 buildings in England that are, or were once, cathedrals, both Anglican and Roman Catholic. A cathedral is very simply defined as a church, large or small, which contains a bishop's ceremonial chair or throne. The word actually comes from the Greek, and then Latin, word *cathedra,* which means 'chair'. A cathedral is the centre of a bishop's territorial area or 'diocese' – a word that also comes directly from the Greek and Latin word for an administrative sub-division of a province in the later Roman Empire. Both dioceses and provinces were re-introduced into England in the 7th century, and to this day the country is divided into only two provinces – Canterbury and York. The map on page 157 illustrates how the system of dioceses evolved, and was eventually overlain by a completely new and different system of Roman Catholic dioceses in the later 19th and the 20th centuries.

Archaeological evidence

No late Roman cathedrals have yet been found in Britain, but they may one day be excavated as Christian basilicas in London and York or in other important Roman cities such as Lincoln or Cirencester. The earliest post-Roman cathedrals were in Canterbury, Rochester and London, and the history of the Anglo-Saxon cathedrals is very well told by the 7th-century monk, theologian and historian the Venerable Bede in his famous *Ecclesiastical History of the English People.* Remarkably, part of the Anglo-Saxon cathedral at Rochester, which was founded in 604, was excavated in 1888 just outside the north-west corner of the later cathedral. It was a small, apsidal building with a nave that was only 42 feet long by 28 feet wide. Later in the 7th century many of the Anglo-Saxon kingdoms in England became dioceses with a bishop, and cathedrals were built at London for the Middle and East Saxons, Dorchester-upon-Thames and then Winchester for the West Saxons, Leicester for the Middle Angles and Lichfield for the people of Mercia. On the Welsh borderlands, Hereford and Worcester were established in sub-kingdoms, and further north York, Ripon and Hexham acquired cathedral churches. The latter two places were established by the remarkable St Wilfrid, who also founded a cathedral church on the island of Selsey for the South Saxons when he was in exile there. Incredibly, the late 7th-century vaulted crypts beneath St Wilfrid's churches at Ripon and Hexham still survive below the later medieval churches.

By the late Anglo-Saxon period almost all of England was covered by the diocesan system, and places like Durham (in 995) and Exeter (in 1050) had become cathedral cities for the first time. Recent archaeological work has uncovered the foundations of large, late Anglo-Saxon cathedrals at Winchester and Canterbury, as well as a fragment at Wells; but only at Sherborne Abbey does a large upstanding fragment of the Anglo-Saxon cathedral, which was later superseded by Salisbury Cathedral, still survive in the west wall of the present building.

Varying influences – from Lanfranc to the Virgin Mary

After the Norman Conquest in 1066, a brilliant, elderly Italian monk known as Lanfranc was made archbishop of Canterbury. Lanfranc started immediately to rebuild his own cathedral at Canterbury. Over the next half century every other cathedral was rebuilt in the sprawling Romanesque style, characterized by rounded arches and heavy pillars. In addition, many cathedrals were moved to new urban sites, and quite a few – including Rochester and Durham in the 1080s – were converted to monastic cathedrals. England was already unique in Europe in having monastic cathedrals, run by Benedictine monks. Archbishop Lanfranc, a monk himself, increased the number so that about half the cathedrals in England were monastic and half were secular – that is, they were run by priests, called canons, who were not members of a monastic order. Carlisle Cathedral, which was not established until 1133, was unique in that it was run by Augustinian canons.

By the middle of the 12th century, the total rebuilding of the English cathedrals was complete. This soon led, in the later 12th and 13th centuries, to the enlargement and transformation of many of them, particularly their eastern arms. This was done in the new Gothic style, distinguished by its pointed arches, rib vaults and flying buttresses. Some truly remarkable structures were built, starting with the superb new choir and Trinity Chapel at Canterbury

RIGHT: The beautifully rebuilt and restored 1308 shrine of St Alban is a fine example of conservation and restoration techniques.

11

RIGHT: The Virgin Mary, Queen of Heaven, is supported by angels in a roundel (*c.* 1500) of the east bay of Winchester Cathedral's Lady chapel.

BELOW: The initial letter to the Letters Patent granting the former estates of St Swithun's Priory, Winchester, to the new dean and chapter of Winchester Cathedral shows Henry VIII handing the document to William Kingsmill, last prior of St Swithun's and first dean of Winchester.

Cathedral (1175–84). The 13th century was also a time when the Blessed Virgin Mary was taking on a new prominence in the Christian church; many splendid new chapels were built for her cult. A unique achievement was the construction of Salisbury Cathedral – a totally new cathedral on a new site; and it is surely no accident that this cathedral was, like Chartres Cathedral in France, dedicated to the Virgin.

Building boom and bust

A high point was reached in the early 14th century when some daring structures were erected, such as the Ely octagon and lantern and the spire of Salisbury Cathedral. Even the terrible Black Death of 1348–50, which wiped out a third of England's population, only put a temporary halt to building work. By the later 14th century the rebuilding of the naves in Canterbury and Winchester cathedrals, as well as the nave at Westminster Abbey, was under way using the new English Perpendicular style. This new architectural style was unique to England from 1330 to the 16th century, and was so called because of the rectilinearity of its decorative panelling and tracery. Throughout the 14th century, in fact starting in the early 13th century, York Minster was being transformed on a colossal scale, and the work here was completed only in the later 15th century. By the early 16th century, and just before Henry VIII's great changes and the Reformation, the building projects were at last coming to an end, and some of the last works were the building of huge towers like those at Durham or Canterbury.

After the Dissolution of the Monasteries, all the monastic cathedrals were refounded by Henry VIII in 1541. These cathedrals, which were given a dean and canons for the first time, are called 'New Foundations'. One monastic cathedral, Coventry, was demolished and six other old monasteries became cathedrals. Virtually no new building work took place. Only after the Great Fire of London, in 1666, reduced the largest cathedral in Britain to a burnt-out shell, was a completely new St Paul's Cathedral designed and built by English architect Sir Christopher Wren (1632–1723).

The later 18th century saw the cathedrals at best sleeping and neglected, and at worst being 'vandalized'. The results of this destruction can still be seen inside places such as Hereford or Salisbury, though of course much worse was to happen in France after the Revolution of 1789–94 when entire cathedrals and abbeys were demolished. Revival in the 19th century started slowly, but from the Age of Reform, new cathedrals and dioceses were created, starting with Ripon in 1836. This gathered pace in the later 19th century, when large parish churches in great conurbations such as Manchester, Newcastle and Wakefield became cathedrals, as well as one huge ancient abbey, St Alban's. Only at remote Truro was a new cathedral built. Alongside this, almost all of England's great medieval cathedrals were being restored and given new life. In the very middle of the 19th century, a completely new diocesan

system of Roman Catholic cathedrals was set up, and some quite large churches were built. Unfortunately for them little money for building work was available, and none of the new cathedrals can be said to be great works of architecture, though the Gothic revivalist, A. W. N. Pugin (1812–52), tried hard.

The 20th century and beyond

At the beginning of the 20th century a huge new Anglican cathedral was started in Liverpool, while several more parish churches were raised to cathedral status. This process of creating new dioceses continued after the First World War, and two new Roman Catholic dioceses, at Brentwood and Lancaster, were also created. One completely new cathedral, at Guildford, was started in 1936, while several other Anglican cathedrals, such as Sheffield and Portsmouth, started to enlarge their existing buildings. The Second World War curtailed all of this, and only in the 1960s was work at last completed on the new Guildford Cathedral, whilst Portsmouth was not finished until the 1990s. By this time architectural ideas had changed, as can be most clearly seen at Sheffield, which is a very strange mixture of styles.

Similarly, the vast new Roman Catholic cathedral at Liverpool, which was started before the Second World War, ended up having a radi-

cally different design when work was renewed in the 1960s. Liturgical changes brought about by the Second Vatican Council, caused centrally placed altars to be universally needed. Perhaps the most liturgically successful of the new Roman Catholic cathedrals was Bristol's Clifton Cathedral. Unfortunately, all the old 19th-century Roman Catholic cathedrals were reordered at the same time, and this led to much destruction of fine 19th-century furnishings. Some Anglican cathedrals were also 'refurnished' at this time, and many fine Victorian fittings were removed. The worst example is perhaps Salisbury where Sir George Gilbert Scott's fine wrought-iron screen, high altar, reredos and tiled floors were destroyed in 1960, leaving the cathedral virtually open from end to end. Chichester Cathedral, by contrast, was furnished at this period with some fine new works of art, and given back its choir screen.

Conservation is now the order of the day, and some excellent work has been undertaken at both Anglican and Roman Catholic cathedrals, such as Winchester and Nottingham. It is ironic, however, that Hereford's beautiful wrought-iron screen, removed in 1967, has just been conserved and reconstructed at great cost for display at the Victoria and Albert Museum.

Tim Tatton-Brown

MEDIEVAL MONASTIC

By the early 12th century, eight fine new monastic cathedrals had been built in England. Although each had the cathedral's bishop as its nominal head, the monasteries were in fact run by the bishop's deputy, the prior, hence the monastic buildings were usually called priories. These cathedrals can, in most cases, be recognized today by the remaining traces of their former monastic buildings – chapter house, dormitory, refectory, etc. – around a cloister. The choirs in these cathedrals were built for the monks to perform their services according to the Rule of St Benedict and, because of the number of monks, the choirs were often large. It is also noticeable that virtually all of this group of cathedrals created large shrines in the cathedrals' eastern arms, which were destroyed by Henry VIII *c.* 1538. After 1541 all of these cathedrals, except Bath (which became a parish church) and Coventry (which was knocked down), were refounded by the king, and given a dean and canons. The first of the new canons were often former monks. Henry VIII also founded new schools at these cathedrals, still called 'The King's School'. Carlisle, the one exception, was built as an Augustinian priory church in the early 12th century.

ABOVE: This carved relief, found on the vault of the east cloister walk at Canterbury Cathedral, may possibly be of Henry Yevele, the late 14th-century royal master mason. RIGHT: The grand west front of Winchester Cathedral has a triple porch that was built *c.* 1360, while the rest – including the great west window – was not built until the 1390s.

CANTERBURY

KENT

ABOVE: This decorative and complex fan vault, designed by John Wastell, can be found below Bell Harry tower.

FAR RIGHT: A single burning candle, placed on the bare flagstones of the Trinity Chapel, marks the site of the shrine of St Thomas Becket. In the foreground is the porphyry pavement (c. 12th century) and on the left is the tomb of Henry IV.

RIGHT: The effigy of Archbishop Chichele (1414–43), the founder of All Souls College, Oxford. The college still pays for the upkeep of his tomb – hence the colourful effigy, which was repainted in the 20th century.

he magnificent cathedral at Canterbury is not only the most important cathedral in England, but it is arguably also the finest architecturally. Within it are three incomparable spaces: the vast Romanesque crypt, the huge 'French' early Gothic choir and presbytery, and the soaring early Perpendicular (and very English) nave. These are all drawn together at the central crossing and capped by one of the noblest towers in Britain.

Work on the present cathedral started in 1071, under the first Norman archbishop, Lanfranc (an Italian monk and a great scholar), and was finally completed with the great tower in 1500. Nine hundred years before this, the first cathedral had been started on this site, soon after the arrival of the first archbishop, St Augustine, in 597. This Anglo-Saxon cathedral had also grown to a large size by the early 11th century, and the foundations of a large western apse were revealed under the nave floor in 1993, flanked by hexagonal stair-turrets. This cathedral was destroyed by fire in 1067, and work on a completely new one, built especially for the monks, was started four years afterwards.

The Norman cathedral

The new cathedral, which was modelled on William the Conqueror's own great abbey in Caen, was built in only seven years (1071–7), and at the same time a large new Benedictine monastery was built on its north side. A decade later this monastery was the largest in England, with 150 monks; and from 1096 a vast new eastern arm was added to the cathedral to house a huge new monks' choir and presbytery. The new choir was built on a very large crypt, at the centre of which was the chapel of Our Lady of the Undercroft. This crypt, one of the largest in Western Europe, is still largely intact with wonderful, late 11th-century carved

capitals and columns; it was created in the time of St Anselm (1093–1109), one of the greatest archbishops of Canterbury. The new choir was consecrated in 1130, after it had been filled with painted (stained) glass, wall-paintings and marble pavements. The towers of this eastern arm were finally completed in the mid-12th century, and these were also covered externally in much fine carved stonework. Soon afterwards, however, two very dramatic events took place in the cathedral: the murder of Archbishop Thomas Becket on 29 December 1170 and the complete gutting of the eastern arm by fire on 5 September 1174. Out of the ashes of this devastation arose, in only nine years, an even more magnificent choir and presbytery, the latter being enlarged to contain, in a new Trinity chapel, a truly magnificent shrine to St Thomas. From this time until 1538, when it was destroyed by Henry VIII, the shrine was the most important in north-western Europe.

The translation of St Thomas

The new choir and presbytery were built in the new French (Gothic) style, and the large space created by the master masons, William of Sens and William the Englishman, is still the finest in the cathedral. It is covered by magnificent ribbed vaults, beneath which are superbly carved great Corinthian capitals surmounted by pointed arches and masses of Purbeck marble shafting. At the very end of the 12th and the beginning of the 13th centuries, under kings Richard and John, there was a period of anarchy in Canterbury; it was not until 1220 that the magnificent shrine itself was completed, and the body of St Thomas could be moved there (or 'translated') from its original burial place in the crypt. This great translation on 7 July 1220 was one of the most splendid events ever seen in medieval England.

After this the cathedral remained largely unaltered for a century and a half, until Edward, the Black Prince (eldest son of Edward III), was allowed to build a new double chantry chapel in the south-eastern part of the crypt in 1363. The transformation of this quite small area (now the French Protestant church in Canterbury) into an early Perpendicular space, with lierne vaults and carved bosses, is another masterpiece, though in miniature. The burial of the Black Prince in the cathedral, after a splendid funeral in 1376, led in the following year to the demolition of the 'outdated' early

ABOVE: The cathedral and chapter house, as seen from the west, dominate the small east Kent town of Canterbury.

LEFT: Canterbury's great Perpendicular nave has a 19th-century pulpit, from where the archbishop still preaches his Easter and Christmas sermons, and a carved screen depicting kings of England. Beyond the open doorway the shrine of St Thomas could be seen.

RIGHT: Late 12th-century stained glass decorates the ambulatory around the shrine. The brightly coloured scenes depict the miracles of the cathedral's own saint, Thomas, and his original tomb in the crypt.

Norman nave and its total rebuilding over the next quarter of a century. This superb nave, which is completely separated from the choir by a great flight of steps and a large stone screen, is yet another work of genius, designed by the royal master mason, Henry Yevele. Its very tall piers and high lierne vaults are lit by enormous windows in the side aisles.

After a slight pause in 1381–2, when the archbishop, Simon of Sudbury, was murdered in the Peasants' Revolt and the cathedral was hit by a severe earthquake, the work continued to completion in 1405. The final stage of this phase, the nave vault, was partly paid for by the new usurping king, Henry IV, and it was he who asked to be buried in the cathedral, on the north side of the shrine of St Thomas; he died in 1413. Ironically this was on the opposite side from the tomb of the Black Prince, whose son, Richard II, Henry IV deposed in 1399.

The rebuilding continues
Most of the other areas of the western part of the cathedral (the towers and transepts) were

This late 11th-century capital, adorned with carvings of mythical beasts, can be found on a supporting pillar in the crypt.

RIGHT: Through the very dark late 11th-century crypt one can glimpse the late 14th-century chapel of Our Lady of the Undercroft, where the Black Prince requested in his will to be buried. However, he was eventually buried on the south side of the shrine of St Thomas.

BELOW: The early 13th-century archiepiscopal throne, made of Purbeck marble, is still used for the enthronement of archbishops of Canterbury.

rebuilt in the Perpendicular style during the 15th century, with a pause during the Wars of the Roses. The splendid new south-west tower (for bells) and porch and a fine new south transept were completed first, followed by the north transept or 'Martyrdom' – the spot where Becket was actually murdered – in the 1470s. This very sacred space, which contained the Altar of the Swordpoint and many tombs, was flanked on the east by a new Lady chapel, where polyphonic Lady Masses were sung by a new boys' and men's choir (the forerunner of the present choir).

All this work was completed in the 1490s with the building of a magnificent new tower over the crossing. This was paid for by the archbishop, John Morton, who was also Henry VII's Lord Chancellor. To start with, a lantern tower, similar to that on York Minster, was built, but in 1493 the archbishop was given a cardinal's cap by the infamous Borgia pope, Alexander VI. This gift led to a change of mind, and the archbishop built a huge double-storey tower, now known as 'Bell Harry' tower after the curfew bell atop the tower, which is still tolled each day. This magnificent structure, whose upper stage is built in red brick, with a Caen stone facing, is

covered on its angle turrets with Morton's rebus and monograms, interspersed with cardinal's caps. 'Capping' his cathedral was Morton's way of showing off. The designer of this magnificent structure was another great master mason, John Wastell, who is most famous for his work at King's College Chapel, Cambridge. Wastell completed the work on the tower by hanging a fan vault beneath it, similar in style to the fan vaults in King's College Chapel. With the completion of this work in 1503 under William Warham, the last archbishop before the Reformation, the rebuilding of the cathedral was finished (though a new north-west tower, replacing the early Norman one, was built as late as 1832). Since that time, 500 years, ago, Canterbury Cathedral has remained one of the greatest works of architecture in Britain.

Inside the building are many other smaller masterpieces, such as the early stained glass, the wall-paintings and the splendid series of archiepiscopal tombs. Outside the nave to the north is a magnificent vaulted cloister with the largest single display of medieval heraldry in England; surrounding this is the best preserved and largest collection of Benedictine monastic buildings in Britain.

WINCHESTER
HAMPSHIRE

ike Canterbury, Winchester was always a very wealthy cathedral, and it likewise had very large sums of money spent on its fabric between the late 11th and early 16th centuries. Consequently the cathedral still contains some magnificent architectural spaces, such as the enormous Perpendicular nave, which is by far the longest nave in Britain; the so-called retrochoir, with its splendid free-standing chantry chapels around the now-gone shrine of St Swithun; and the beautiful eastern Lady chapel. There is also some marvellous Norman architecture in the transepts, though it was originally planned for these to be rebuilt and 'modernized', as occurred in the presbytery, in the early 16th century.

Winchester was also one of the least stable cathedrals in England, unlike its near neighbour Salisbury, so the original crossing tower fell in 1107, and the upper parts of the transepts and eastern arm were never completed. The cathedral was in fact built on a sloping site in the middle of a ruined Roman city that also had a rising water table (the Norman crypts are now almost always flooded in winter). The eastern arm was only finally saved from collapse by large-scale underpinning of the foundations, using a diver, in the early 20th century.

ABOVE RIGHT: The Epiphany chapel houses a series of windows designed in stained glass by Edward Burne-Jones, including this Annunciation.

Early history
The first cathedral was built by King Cenwalh of Wessex in the mid-7th century, and its site is now marked out on the ground immediately to the north of the nave. Most of the remaining foundations of this ancient building, known as the Old Minster, and of its late Anglo-Saxon enlargements, were excavated in the 1960s.

When the relics of the most famous of the early bishops of Winchester, St Swithun (died 862), were moved from outside the Old Minster to a new internal shrine on 15 July 971, it rained for the next 40 days, giving rise to the later myth about the English summer. In the late 10th century, when Winchester had effectively become the capital of England, the old secular canons were thrown out of the cathedral by their powerful monk-bishop, St Æthelwold – a close colleague of St Dunstan, archbishop of Canterbury – and replaced by a group of Benedictine monks.

LEFT: Wood carvings, such as this falconer with his charge, can be seen in the spandrels above the early 14th-century choir stalls.

DEDICATION
- Cathedral Church of the Holy Trinity, and of St Peter and St Paul and of St Swithun

HISTORY
- First cathedral, the Old Minster, built in the mid-7th century
- Benedictine priory from late 10th century to 1539
- Building of Norman cathedral started in 1079
- Present cathedral completed c. 1525
- Shrine of St Swithun destroyed in 1538
- Jane Austen buried here in 1817
- Cathedral underpinned 1905–12

OF SPECIAL INTEREST
- Site of Anglo-Saxon cathedral north of the nave
- Early Norman crypt, transepts and crossing tower
- Mid-12th-century Tournai marble font
- Medieval wall-paintings in Holy Sepulchre chapel
- Thirteenth-century floor tiles in the eastern arm
- Large episcopal chantry chapels in eastern arm and nave
- Early 14th-century choir stalls and canopies
- Great 15th-century image screen behind the high altar
- Remodelled early 16th-century Lady chapel

The present building was started by another powerful bishop, Walkelin, in 1079, and, unlike Canterbury, it was from the beginning meant to be on a very large scale indeed. Its proportions were roughly based on Old St Peter's in Rome, and in its time it was perhaps the largest building north of the Alps. Even today, shorn of its Norman western towers but with an enlarged Lady chapel, it is, at 556 feet long, the longest cathedral in Europe. The eastern arm of the Norman cathedral, which as usual was started first, has been replaced, but its plan can still be seen in the Norman crypts beneath.

There was a small eastern apsidal chapel that abutted a large semicircular ambulatory around the high altar. The relics of St Swithun were enshrined behind the high altar. The monks' choir was under the crossing tower and extended westwards into the immense 12-bay nave, as it still does today. On either side of the choir and crossing are two very large double-aisled transepts, where the monumental early Norman architecture is still visible. The outer corners of these transepts were designed to be capped by their own small towers, but these were never completed – probably due to stability problems. The Norman shell of the nave still survives behind much of the Perpendicular work, but it is necessary to go up into the triforium to see this early work. At the west end were two large towers, and, though these were demolished in the 14th century, part of the core of the south side of one can still be seen in the later boundary wall. As mentioned, early in the 12th century the low crossing tower had to be rebuilt – a myth says that this was because the wicked King William Rufus had been buried beneath it – and there is also some fine mid-12th-century decorative work on the west side of the south transept. The wonderful black Tournai marble font in the nave is of the same date.

Very early in the 13th century a large new eastern arm was started, but this also quickly became unstable, and the upper stages were never finished. Today it is a fine space, rather like an aisled hall, which contains a wonderful series of chantry chapels for various late medieval and early Tudor bishops. This space, inaccurately called the retrochoir, was clearly designed to house a new shrine to St Swithun (following the model set by Canterbury), but the translation of the relics from just behind the high altar did not actually take place until

ABOVE: The west front of
Winchester Cathedral is a fine
example of the Perpendicular
style of architecture, with a
Norman tower behind.

TOP LEFT: The north aisle of the
crypt, particularly when
flooded, is a fantastically
eerie location for *Sound II*,
the contemporary sculpture
by Antony Gormley.

BOTTOM LEFT: The ornate mid-
12th-century Tournai marble
font in the nave is decorated
with scenes from the legend
of St Nicholas.

1476. To the east of the retrochoir is the Lady chapel, which was remodelled in the late 15th century. It still has an excellent mixture of 13th- and 15th-century architecture in its side walls, as well as fine wooden stalls and a western screen. The neighbouring chapel to the south was remodelled in the 1490s for yet another chantry chapel, this time for Bishop Thomas Langton (1493–1501).

The nave rebuilt

The complete rebuilding of the huge nave after 1394 by the famous bishop William of Wykeham was by far the largest architectural work at Winchester in the later Middle Ages. Wykeham's predecessor, Bishop Edington, had, however, already started work at the west end, just before his death in 1366, by demolishing the old Romanesque west towers and building the fine triple porch. After Edington's death, work on the west front continued for at least five years under his successor, William of Wykeham, who became bishop in 1367. The first phase of Wykeham's work involved rebuilding the lower part of the west front and the aisle walls of the two western bays of the nave. There was then a pause of about 20 years, during which time the bishop set up and built his two famous educational establishments, Winchester College and New College, Oxford. Then in 1393 Bishop Wykeham ordered the prior to recommence the work on the nave, and soon afterwards he agreed to fund the whole of the work himself. There followed a decade of concentrated work under the royal master mason, William Wynford, during which the whole of the south side of the nave was transformed. At the time of Wykeham's

ABOVE: This exceptionally fine wall-painting of the deposition and entombment of Christ has survived in the Holy Sepulchre chapel, almost intact, from the 12th century.

LEFT: The unaltered Norman north transept illustrates what the huge nave was like before its remodelling in the 14th century.

RIGHT: The modern batik banners that decorate the nave all the way down to the choir screen were designed by Thetis Blacker.

death in 1404, work was already under way on the north side, and the bishop's remarkable will, written the previous year, laid down the blueprint for the future. By the time of his death Wykeham had also had his own chantry chapel built on the south side of the nave.

The work on the nave, including the building of the remarkable high vaults, then continued more slowly for perhaps another half century before it was finally completed under Bishop William Waynflete (1447–86). This bishop and his predecessor, Cardinal Henry Beaufort (1405–47), built themselves magnificent chantry chapels in the retrochoir, but the final remodelling work in the presbytery was not undertaken until the early 16th century, when Bishop Fox (1500–28) paid for the work in the aisles and for the new wooden vault over the presbytery. He also built himself a chantry chapel, as did his successor, Stephen Gardiner.

DURHAM
DURHAM

DURHAM

DEDICATION

- Cathedral Church of Christ and the Blessed Virgin Mary

HISTORY

- The 'White Church' completed in 998 for St Cuthbert's body
- Present Norman cathedral built from 1093 to 1133
- Shrine of St Cuthbert, behind the high altar 1104–1538
- Western Galilee chapel built as Lady chapel c. 1175
- New eastern arm ('Nine Altars') built in the mid-13th century
- Norman chapter house demolished in 1796, rebuilt in 1895

OF SPECIAL INTEREST

- Sanctuary ring on north door
- Seventh-century coffin, pectoral cross and other remains from tomb of St Cuthbert (now in the Undercroft Museum)
- The Venerable Bede's tomb in the Galilee porch (his body was brought to Durham in 1022)
- Neville screen (made in London c. 1380) behind the high altar
- Bishop's throne over Bishop Hatfield's tomb (c. 1380)
- Late 15th-century astronomical clock
- Late 17th-century font and large canopy
- Cloister and monastic buildings to the south of the cathedral

ABOVE: The tomb of the Venerable Bede, which dates from 1542, lies in the Galilee chapel.

RIGHT: The famous 12th-century bronze sanctuary ring on the north door of the nave is actually a replica – the original is in the Undercroft Museum. Those seeking sanctuary would have held on to the ring for protection.

FAR RIGHT: The cathedral's south-west side is well protected today by rich woodland. Above the tree tops the cathedral's tall towers protrude to dominate the Old Mill on the River Wear.

urham Cathedral is famous throughout England for three things: its incomparable setting, its magnificent Romanesque architecture and St Cuthbert. The present cathedral, which was started in 1093, sits high up on a rocky mound almost entirely surrounded by trees and the River Wear. The trees are relatively new (they would not have been here in medieval times), but this very strategic site was discovered just over a thousand years ago by a group of monks, who were carrying the coffin and relics of St Cuthbert and looking for a place of safety from the Vikings. Cuthbert became bishop of Lindisfarne long before this in 685, and when he died two years later on the Farne Islands, he was buried at Lindisfarne.

The foundation of Durham

Two hundred years after Cuthbert's death the north-east coast of England was constantly being raided by the Vikings, so the monks went inland, first to Chester-le-Street, and then in 995 to Durham, for greater security. At Durham a new monastery was founded, and a new church called the 'White Church' was completed and dedicated in 998. After the Norman Conquest a large new castle was erected from 1071, to the north of the church to block the landward side of the peninsula. The castle was for the bishop, William of St Calais, who in 1080 became the first prince-bishop under King William the Conqueror. This made him both the military and spiritual leader of the extreme north of England at a time when the Normans were consolidating their power on the Scottish border. Bishop William, who was a Norman monk, founded a new 'reformed' Benedictine monastery at Durham in 1083, and a decade later, on 29 July 1093, he started the construction of the present cathedral to replace the 'White Church'. A contemporary chronicle gives some indication of how the work proceeded, and we are told that when Ranulf Flambard became bishop in 1099 the church had been made 'as far as the nave'. On 29 August 1104 the remains of St Cuthbert were translated to a new resting place at the east end of the cathedral – behind

the high altar in the eastern apse – and by this time the stone vault was probably complete over the eastern arm. This vault started to crack in 1235 and was replaced by the present vault soon afterwards. By the time of Flambard's death in 1128 the walls were complete 'up to the covering' (this perhaps refers to the stone vault), and in the next five years work on the nave was completed. Durham Cathedral was therefore the earliest church to be covered completely in stone vaults, and much of this vaulting in the transepts and nave still survives. It was supported by early proto-flying buttresses, which can still be seen above the aisle vaults and under the triforium roofs.

The monks then continued building their own monastic offices – chapter house, dormitory, etc. – before the new bishop, Hugh Le Puiset (1154–95), paid for the magnificent Galilee chapel at the western end of the cathedral. It was, in fact, a Lady chapel with five aisles, but it also acted as a porch. Apparently work on an earlier Lady chapel had started in the more usual place at the east end of the cathedral, but this had failed due to structural problems. An amusing myth suggests that this was because St Cuthbert, a misogynist, did not want a chapel for a woman (even the Virgin Mary!) so close to his place of burial. The Galilee chapel is superbly placed on the cliff top, adjoining the twin western towers and the three west doorways of the cathedral (the central doorway was later blocked by the altar to the Virgin). Inside it are wonderful chevroned arcades, and the vertical monolithic shafts in the piers are of Purbeck marble, the stone's most northerly use in England. This chapel also now contains the tomb of the Venerable Bede, whose remains had been brought to Durham in the early 11th century.

Bishop Poore's vision

Early in the 13th century the upper stages of the very substantial western towers were built, but soon afterwards there were structural problems in the eastern vaults above the shrine.

BELOW LEFT: The attractive 20th-century tester that hangs above the site of the shrine of St Cuthbert was designed by Arts and Crafts architect Sir Ninian Comper (1864–1960).

BELOW RIGHT: The wonderful Galilee chapel has chevroned arches and monolithic Purbeck marble shafts.

Richard Poore (1228–37) was the unfortunate bishop who had to deal with these problems. He had been translated, against his wishes, from Salisbury, where he had been presiding over the building of the city's new cathedral.

Poore's idea for Durham was to have a large new eastern transept with nine altars, which would also allow the area around the back of the shrine to be opened up. Poore seems to have conceived of this plan in Salisbury, as it closely resembles that cathedral's greater transept (which had been laid out in the 1220s). A similar great eastern transept with nine altars was built at Fountains Abbey.

It is thought that, as well as ideas, Poore also brought masons with him from Salisbury. However, because of Durham's structural problems, truly massive foundations and buttresses had to be built, and the work on this fine new 'hammer head' to the cathedral was not finished until the 1250s. Even thereafter work seems to have continued, perhaps for towers at either end of the transept. These were, however, never finished. Sadly, the shrine of St Cuthbert was broken up and destroyed on Henry VIII's orders in 1540, but the worn paving around it is still medieval.

After the building of the great eastern transept at Durham, only more minor works were undertaken in the later Middle Ages. A great west window was inserted in about 1341, and a wonderful stone screen (the Neville Screen) was made in London of Caen stone and brought up to Durham to be put behind the high altar in 1380. At the end of the 15th century a large new lantern tower was built over the crossing, and after a slight pause an upper stage was added, making Durham Cathedral even more prominent on its rock. Early in the 16th century there were even plans to add a spire.

To the south of the cathedral a fine set of monastic buildings still survives around a large cloister. The great dormitory, rebuilt on the west side of the cloister from 1398 to 1404,

now contains the library, while the deanery in the south-east corner is adapted from the earlier prior's lodging. Sadly the chapter house was destroyed in the late 18th-century 'restoration' of Bishop Shute Barrington (using James Wyatt as his architect). It was rebuilt a century later, in a late Victorian restoration. Luckily Wyatt's other plans, including the destruction of the Galilee porch, were never carried out.

ABOVE: The massive piers in the nave support the triforium and the famous ribbed vaults; each pier is made up of small, deeply carved decorative blocks. In the distance is the great rose window at the centre of the chapel of the Nine Altars.

ELY

CAMBRIDGESHIRE

ABOVE: Superb early
14th-century carved
work can be found in
the Lady chapel. Sadly,
many such details
were damaged during
the Reformation
when the Lady
chapel became a
parish church.

BELOW: The Isle of Ely, in
the wonderfully peace-
ful fens, is dominated
by its great cathedral.

n the late Anglo-Saxon period, Ely was, along with Canterbury, Glastonbury and Winchester, one of the most powerful Benedictine monasteries in England. It was first founded in 673 by St Etheldreda (or Audrey, as the saint was called later), but was sacked by the Vikings in 870. A new monastic church was consecrated in 970 by Æthelwold, the great monk-bishop of Winchester, and the abbey's vast estates were spread widely in East Anglia. In 1083 the elderly Abbot Simeon, previously prior of Winchester (and Bishop Walkelin's brother), started to build a very large monastic church, partly modelled on Winchester. Simeon died in 1093; by 1106 the eastern arm was complete enough to allow a translation of St Etheldreda. Not far away to the east, another great Benedictine abbey was also being rebuilt at Bury St Edmunds, and it was unclear where the new cathedrals for East Anglia were to be situated. In 1095, however, the see was moved from Thetford to the city of Norwich, and this became the new cathedral city. But this was not the end of the story: in 1109 most of Cambridgeshire was taken away from the huge Lincoln diocese to form the new, quite small, diocese of Ely, with Hervey (a former bishop of Bangor) as the first bishop.

A Norman triumph

As is usual, the eastern arm of the Norman abbey church has gone (replaced in the 13th and 14th centuries), but it seems to have had a central apse and no crypt. The large aisled transepts do survive, and these are now the earliest remaining parts of the fabric, with great Norman piers, cushion capitals and round arches as in Winchester. The north-west

corner of the north transept collapsed in 1699, and was rebuilt with a new door based on Wren's door for St Mary-le-Bow in London.

The most spectacular survival from the early Norman church is the wonderful 12-bay nave with its compound piers, large triforium and clerestory. With the replacement of Winchester's nave in the 14th century and the destruction of the nave of St Paul's in 1666, this is now the most splendid early Norman nave in England. It is 72 feet high and 230 feet long, and beyond is an unusually large western transept with its own eastern chapel. The west end of the cathedral was completed at the end of the 12th century with outer corner turrets and a great central tower to which a spire was added in 1230. The spire was removed in the late 14th century when an upper stage was added to the top of the tower, and although the north side of the west transept had collapsed in the 15th century, the west end of Ely Cathedral is still a splendid sight – not least for the large, added 13th-century Galilee porch and great chamber above.

Between 1234 and 1252 the bishop, Hugh Northwold, paid for a very fine new addition to the eastern arm. This was to surround a large new shrine for St Etheldreda, and to allow a row of five new chapels to be made against the east wall. The eastern façade had developed out of the new 'Early English' work at Salisbury and is contemporary with the 'Nine Altars' transept at Durham. When the work was finished in 1252, the cathedral was 537 feet long and complete as a structure.

In pursuit of excellence

In the early 14th century some of the most spectacular and daring architecture ever created – such as the tower and spire of Salisbury Cathedral – was produced for the richest of the great ecclesiastical establishments, and the work at Ely Cathedral is perhaps the best example of all.

In 1321 the bishop, prior and sacrist (a senior monk in charge of the fabric) decided that a really fine new Lady chapel was needed, so the foundations were laid out and construction was started on a completely separate new rectangular building, 100 feet long by 46 feet

RIGHT: The great Norman nave as seen from the north side of the octagon. In medieval times, the monks' choir stalls would have been in the foreground.

ABOVE: Mid- to late 12th-century arcading decorates the south-west corner of the cathedral. This wonderful, late Romanesque decoration originally extended right across the west front of the cathedral, but unfortunately the northern half collapsed in the 15th century.

smashed woodwork cleared away. Then, in a moment of inspired genius, he decided not to rebuild the tower, but instead to remove all traces of the old crossing and build a larger irregular octagon.

This wonderful new space, lit by fine Decorated windows in the angles, was constructed over the following six years. The next, and most difficult, stage was to roof the area, which was 72 feet across. Luckily the royal master carpenter, William Hurley, was able to devise a clever system of hammer-beam trusses and ring beams to create the timber lantern over the crossing that is still today the most spectacular element in the cathedral. As this carpentry work was going ahead, the bishop paid for wonderful new carved arcades at the west end of the presbytery, now rather hidden by the choir stalls. Above this was even finer Decorated tracery in the triforium – now partly filled with organ pipes – and the clerestory. Then, as if this was not enough, the sacrist returned to rebuilding the separate Lady chapel. This fabulous building, which looks superficially like a chapter house, was saved after the Reformation by being turned into a new parish church. However, all the statues, many of the fine figures in the carved decoration and the stained glass were smashed, and it is much more difficult now to appreciate what a miniature 'paradise' the inside of the building was like before the Reformation. The whole building was designed to be a celebration of the Blessed Virgin Mary, with intricate decoration and colour everywhere, and it was here that all the monks could sit in their wonderful canopied seats to celebrate the life of the Virgin.

Work on the Lady chapel was then affected by yet another catastrophe: the Black Death of 1348–50, which killed many of the monks. Most of the work was complete by this time – and the Lady altar was dedicated in 1353 – but the great east and west windows, and perhaps the amazing stone vault which spans 46 feet, were not completed until 1375.

With all this hard work in the 14th century, the monks never got round to rebuilding the nave (unlike at Canterbury, Winchester, Worcester and Bath), and this is surely to our gain. They did, however, rebuild the north part of the western transept after yet another collapse.

Two final miniature works of architecture should also be mentioned here: the fantastic

wide, to the north of the presbytery. Its south-west corner just adjoined the north-east corner of the north transept. On 22 February 1322, just as work on the walls was about to get under way, a catastrophe occurred. The great central tower collapsed, destroying all of the monks' choir stalls below the crossing and wrecking the three bays of the Norman chancel to the east. A contemporary chronicle records that Alan of Walsingham, the sacrist, was so overcome that at first he did not know where to turn or what to do. He soon pulled himself together, however, and had the rubble and chantry chapels of Bishop Alcock (died 1501) and Bishop West (died 1534). These two chapels are in the extreme north-east and south-east corners of the cathedral, and in many ways they are even more elaborate than the episcopal chapels in Winchester Cathedral. Bishop Alcock's chantry, which was begun in 1488, is the more elaborate, with canopy after canopy being created under a spectacular open-work pendant vault. Bishop West's chantry, which was built in 1525–33, is more restrained, but here there are early Renaissance motifs and a wonderful panelled vault, details that were also appearing in the contemporary Hampton Court Palace, and particularly in its chapel.

RIGHT: The spectacular timber vaults over the octagon are surmounted by the lantern, which has its own timber vault above. At the top and bottom of the photograph are the early 15th-century false hammer-beam roofs in the transepts.

BELOW: The 13th-century eastern arm is fitted out with 19th-century furnishings, including the high altar, the reredos and the marble floor, on which is marked the site of the shrine of St Etheldreda. The original fittings were destroyed during the reordering of the presbytery in the late 18th century.

NORWICH
NORFOLK

ABOVE: This 'Green Man' on a boss in the east cloister walk is a superbly carved human face with hawthorn leaves protruding from it.

FAR RIGHT: The apsidal east end of the great triforium has, above the Norman arcading, large 14th-century clerestory windows and a magnificent 15th-century high vault.

RIGHT: Another spectacular vault boss, with Christ on the Cross between the Virgin Mary and John, the beloved disciple.

t the time of the Norman Conquest the see for East Anglia was based at North Elmham. Not long afterwards it was moved to Thetford, where it remained for about 20 years (1075–95). The Domesday Book, however, suggests that by the early 1080s the building of a new cathedral at Norwich was already intended, though the official move did not happen until 1095. The next year the bishop, Herbert de Losinga, a Norman monk, who had earlier been prior of Fécamp in Normandy, formally laid out the foundations, and yet another huge new Norman cathedral was erected in the following half century.

A monument to Norman brilliance

Norwich Cathedral is still one of the largest and most complete Romanesque great churches in the country: almost the entire skeleton of the Norman building survives. Particularly noticeable is the eastern arm, which, despite remodelling in the 14th and 15th centuries, still retains its original ambulatory and some of its semicircular chapels. The easternmost chapel was demolished in the mid-13th century and replaced by a larger, rectangular Lady chapel. Unfortunately, this in turn was demolished in the later 16th century, to be replaced with a new smaller eastern chapel only in 1930. With the addition of the Lady chapel the cathedral was about 490 feet long, and its 14-bay nave of about 260 feet is also one of the longest in England. The initial plan of the eastern arm followed that of Herbert's own abbey in Fécamp, and its transepts (unlike those of Winchester and Ely) are relatively small. The huge nave, which was built between 1121 and 1145, was perhaps meant to rival the nave of the vast abbey at Bury St Edmunds, but unlike Bury and Ely it did not acquire a grandiose towered west front. Norwich never housed the shrine of a major saint, and this is perhaps another reason why the eastern arm was not rebuilt on a large scale in the 13th century.

A unique survival at Norwich is the bishop's throne or *cathedra*, fragments of which can be seen behind the high altar in the apse. The very worn fragments of the carved arms of the throne, which perhaps date back to Norman times (though an earlier Anglo-Saxon date has also been suggested), were restored and reset on a new semicircular stepped

ABOVE: The magnificent 15th-century lierne vault at the east end of the nave above the choir. The organ case was completed only after the end of the Second World War.

ABOVE RIGHT: An unusual incised pillar on the south side of the nave, similar to those found in Durham Cathedral. This view looks west to Bishop Nix's chantry chapel, which was built across the south aisle.

dais in 1959. Canterbury still has an axial throne of the early 13th century behind the high altar, while most other cathedrals usually only retain their later medieval thrones, on the south side of the presbytery.

Externally the most striking feature of the Romanesque cathedral is the very large mid-12th-century crossing tower. This is covered in a unique decorative scheme of roundels and arcading between prominent shafted corner turrets. In the 1290s a large timber and lead spire was added to the top of the tower, but this was blown down onto the presbytery in a great storm in 1362. A replacement spire was burnt by lighting in 1463,

while the present fine structure, which is made of brick and covered in stone, was built in the 1480s. It is exceptionally slender, and at 315 feet is second only to Salisbury in height.

Disaster strikes

Probably the greatest disaster to befall the cathedral was the riot outside the St Ethelbert Gate in 1272. A dispute between the town and the monks got out of hand when the citizens set fire to the gates and broke into the monastery. The fire quickly spread to the cathedral and monastic buildings, where both the conflagration and the citizens inflicted a great deal of damage. The city was forced to pay the huge sum of £2000 to repair the damage, and 30 of its citizens were hanged. The repair work after 1272 took a long time, and this can perhaps best be seen in the cloister, where the rebuilding of each of the walks continued for many years (1297–1430). The cloister is one of the largest in England (as with the spire, it is second only to Salisbury), and the fine stone vaults of various types over each of the walks are covered in about 400 carved bosses. Many of these depict remarkable little scenes from scripture or mythology. The finest vaults and carved bosses, however, are in the cathedral itself. They were inserted at the very end of the Middle Ages and now cover the whole of the great nave, transepts and presbytery.

Further work started in the mid-15th century, when Bishop Alnwick (1426–36), who died in 1449, left money for a vast nine-light window at the west end of the nave. His successor, Bishop Lyhart (1446–72), carried out the work and paid for the wonderful lierne vault (i.e. with small cross ribs) in the nave, which is of great length and which, from a distance, looks more like a fan vault. A new vault was then installed in the presbytery in the 1480s under Bishop Goldwell (1472–99), and on the south side of the presbytery is the bishop's own chantry chapel and tomb. Goldwell was also responsible for the rebuilding of the spire. The vaulting of the transepts was carried out last, after another fire in 1509, and the work was only finished at the beginning of Henry VIII's reign under Bishop Nix (1501–35). This bishop also built himself a fine chantry chapel on the south side of the nave.

The nave vaults are well lit by the great west window and smaller clerestory and triforium windows, but the presbytery vaults are flooded with light from the very large 14th-century clerestory windows that were put in after the collapse of the spire in 1362. The upper wall is, therefore, thinner here, and large flying buttresses had to be added externally to support the vaults. Elsewhere all the vaults fit perfectly into the much earlier Romanesque masonry.

RIGHT: The great Romanesque tower and 15th-century spire as seen from the ruins of the Hostry hall off the west range of the cloister. The ruined 13th-century doorway and porch are in the foreground.

WORCESTER
WORCESTERSHIRE

ABOVE: Saints Oswald and Wulfstan flank the head of King John on his tomb in the presbytery.

RIGHT: A mass of early Norman columns and cushion capitals in Bishop Wulfstan's large crypt.

FAR RIGHT: The famous view of the cathedral's tower and west front from across the River Severn. The great west window dates from the reign of Queen Victoria.

he new diocese for Worcestershire and Gloucestershire was first created in the late 670s at a time when the remarkable 'Greek' archbishop of Canterbury, Theodore of Tarsus, was creating a series of new bishoprics in England for different tribes and sub-kingdoms. In south-west Mercia he made dioceses for the sub-kingdoms of the Hwicce and the Magonsaettan, based at Worcester and Hereford respectively.

A Benedictine revival

Nothing is known about the early cathedrals, but in 961 the saintly Oswald became bishop of Worcester at a time when Benedictine monasticism was being revived in England under St Dunstan, first at Glastonbury and then at major cathedrals such as Winchester. Bishop Oswald at Worcester followed suit, and in 983 he established a monastic community at a new church of St Mary, which became the cathedral. After his death in 992, Oswald was quickly considered a saint, and his tomb became a place of pilgrimage. The cathedral was unfortunately sacked by the Danes in 1041, but in 1062 another great monk, Wulfstan, became bishop.

Wulfstan was of such stature that he was the only Anglo-Saxon bishop to be left in place after the Norman Conquest. Wulfstan started to build a new Norman cathedral in 1084, and the magnificent large apsidal crypt is perhaps his greatest surviving memorial. Wulfstan was also considered a saint after his death in 1095, and he was formally

canonized by the Pope in 1203. The shrines of the two great bishops were then put just in front, and on either side of, the high altar. Shortly afterwards in 1216, King John was also buried here at his own request. The shrines were, of course, destroyed by Henry VIII, but the magnificent 13th-century effigy of King John, with the figures of saints Oswald and Wulfstan on either side of his head, still survives in front of the high altar. It sits on an elaborate tomb chest made in 1529. Not far away to the south-east is the much more splendid chantry chapel of Prince Arthur, Henry VIII's elder brother, who died at Ludlow Castle in 1502, aged 15 and having just married Catherine of Aragon. The chantry is a superb structure, with almost flat pendant vaults inside, and it was erected in 1504.

Thirteenth-century trends

Soon after King John's funeral in 1216, work started on a fine new Early English eastern arm with smaller eastern transepts and an axial Lady chapel. This was, as at Durham, to allow the area around the two high altar shrines to be opened up for pilgrims, and followed the pattern already set in the new cathedral at Salisbury. Bishop William de Blois (1218–36) was so pleased with the new work that he decided to continue it westwards into the presbytery after demolishing the old Norman work. This area now holds the choir stalls, though in the 13th century the monks' choir was further west under the crossing.

The whole of the work in the cathedral's eastern half was finished by the end of the 13th century, and at this time Bishop Wulfstan's late 11th-century nave must have looked quite out of date. Two bays at the western end of the nave had been rebuilt in the Transitional style in the late 12th century, and this work still survives. All the rest of the nave, however, was rebuilt in stages in the 14th century, and this is a particularly interesting area in which to see how the architectural style changed from the Decorated to the Perpendicular.

Documentary evidence

One of the few contemporary documentary sources for Worcester tells us that Bishop Thomas Cobham (1317–27) 'made the vault of the north aisle in the nave'. This is confirmed not only by the earlier style of vaulting in the eastern three bays of the nave's north aisle, but

ABOVE: King John's tomb presides over the early 13th-century presbytery. Unlike in many cathedrals, the late Victorian high altar, marble screen and fine floor tiles have survived.

LEFT: In the cathedral's choir, 13th-century architecture towers above the Victorian choir stalls, organ and pulpit.

also by the fact that a new external chapel (the Jesus chapel) was built here, apparently as Cobham's chantry chapel. Work then continued westwards on rebuilding the north side of the nave in the 1330s. Earlier writers have suggested that the work was halted by the Black Death in 1348–50. However, more recent research has shown that the new work on the south side of the nave also took place before the Black Death, probably under Prior Wulfstan de Braunsford (1317–49), who became bishop in 1339. This man, alas, also died in the Black Death, but not before most of the work in the nave (though not the vaults) was complete.

Following the Black Death, there was a seven-year pause before the Norman crossing tower was demolished and a new more sturdy structure was erected between 1357 and 1374. After this date, work on installing the stone vaults progressed rapidly, moving from east (under the tower) to west (the west end of the

nave) between 1375 and 1379. We know that new stalls were then made for the monks' choir (many fine stalls with carved misericords survive), and that the new great west window was finished in 1380. The large north porch – the principal entry – was then rebuilt in 1386, before the masons started work on rebuilding the monks' cloister and ten-sided chapter house to the south of the nave.

Unfortunately, Worcester Cathedral suffered from very harsh and unsympathetic restoration in the 18th and 19th centuries, and the present great west window and much of the external masonry is no longer medieval. Much 'scraping' of the exterior took place, as well as the constant removing and adding of windows, buttresses and pinnacles. There were large Perpendicular windows at both the west and east ends of the cathedral, and to the north there was a fine free-standing octagonal bell-tower, with a great timber and lead spire – all have now gone.

ROCHESTER
KENT

ABOVE: The mid-14th-century wall-paintings above the 13th-century choir stalls portray the lion of England and the fleur-de-lys of France.

RIGHT: This remarkably elaborate early 14th-century doorway in the south-east transept leads through to the chapter room and cathedral library.

ochester is a relatively small and little-visited cathedral, but it contains some fine areas of medieval architecture as well as the earliest surviving monastic choir stalls in any cathedral in England. It also has the exceptionally early foundation date of AD 604, when St Augustine sent one of his Roman monks, Justin, to be the first bishop. Equally remarkable, part of the first cathedral was excavated under the north-west corner of the present cathedral in 1889, when the west front was being underpinned.

After the Norman Conquest, Lanfranc, the archbishop of Canterbury, sent his right-hand man, Gundulf, to be bishop in 1077. He then started to build the present cathedral, and in 1083 to establish a new group of Benedictine monks there. The western part of the present crypt, with its plain groin vaults, is still the crypt that was created by Gundulf in the 1080s. Gundulf also built the nave, and, as a man 'very skilled in the use of masonry', helped to build neighbouring Rochester Castle and the Tower of London. On the north side of the cathedral is a tall tower, later known as Gundulf's Tower, which was built as the cathedral's bell-tower in the early 12th century; unfortunately its top was removed

in the early 19th century. Around 1115 a new cloister for the monks was laid out on the south-east side of the cathedral. The remains of the early 12th-century east range (chapter house and dormitory) can still be seen. The lower part of the chapter house façade and the doorway into the dormitory were refaced in the 1160s with more decorative work, including the use of Tournai marble and onyx marble for shafts. At the same time the nave and the west front of the cathedral were being refaced, using beautifully carved Caen stone.

BELOW: Rochester's late 12th-century choir possesses the oldest choir stalls in England, with the back stalls dating from 1227.

A disastrous fire

In 1179 there was a great fire at Rochester, and soon after this a completely new eastern arm, on a crypt and with eastern transepts, was added to the monks' choir. This fine structure was built to contain the new shrines of St Paulinus and St Ithamar on either side of the high altar, and in 1256 it received an additional shrine in the north-east transept for St William of Perth. To the north of this now demolished shrine is the fine tomb of Bishop Walter de Merton, chancellor of England and founder of Merton College, Oxford. The new choir was finally completed in 1227 (the back stalls date from this time), and work continued on the rebuilding of the greater transepts. The south transept always contained the Lady chapel. In the later 13th century work started on rebuilding the nave, but funds ran out after the first two bays were completed and before the side vaults were put in. The springers for these vaults can, however, still be seen. All the main rebuilding work from the late 11th century to 1238 was carried out when Rochester was subservient to Canterbury – the bishop of Rochester, uniquely, was appointed by the archbishop as both his suffragan and as a diocesan bishop. After this the monks were given the right of free election by Pope Gregory IX, but as Rochester was a comparatively poor foundation little extra building took place, although a crossing tower and spire were built in the early 14th century. These were subsequently demolished in 1825 and rebuilt in 1904.

BATH ABBEY

SOMERSET

DEDICATION

- Abbey Church of St Peter and St Paul

HISTORY

- Major Roman city with hot springs, baths and temple
- Monastery from 8th century, reformed by St Dunstan
- Edgar crowned King of England here in 973
- Bishop's *cathedra* moved to the monastic church in 1090
- Bishop Oliver King starts the rebuilding work in 1499
- Becomes the parish church for the city in 1572, and rebuilding starts

OF SPECIAL INTEREST

- Norman fragments at the east end and below the floor
- Fan vaults and Prior Birde's chantry chapel in eastern arm
- Bishop King's west front and 1617 west door
- Bishop Montague's Baroque tomb in the nave
- Many 18th- and 19th-century wall-monuments commemorating fashionable visitors to Georgian and Regency Bath

ABOVE: During the 18th century Bath became a popular spa town. Many of those who came to 'take the waters' were already quite ill and subsequently died in Bath. This influx of people contributed substantially to the abundance of 18th- and early 19th-century memorials found in the Abbey.

his fine building is almost always referred to by the name of Bath Abbey, although it should properly be called Bath Cathedral. There was already an important monastic church in the Roman walled city in the late Anglo-Saxon period, and in 973 Edgar was crowned king of England there. Then, after the Norman Conquest, a man called John de Villula (or John of Tours) became bishop of Wells. Following the trend of the time, de Villula was persuaded by the king to move the see from the 'village' of Wells to the larger town of Bath and to base it in the Benedictine abbey there. This was done in 1090, and soon afterwards he must have started to build a new Norman church. This building had an eastern ambulatory and transepts with a series of apsidal chapels leading off them. A 10-bay nave was then added, which contained the monks' choir; the present church occupies only the site of this nave, the whole of the eastern arm having been demolished in the mid-16th century. A few traces of the old Norman fabric can be seen in the east walls of the present building, as well as below the floor at the west end of the north aisle, where they were uncovered in about 1865. (The Norman ground

RIGHT: Bishop James Montague's (1608–15) tomb rests on the north side of the nave. Above the tomb, in the north aisle, are fine fan vaults dating from the 19th century.

level is about 4 feet below the present floor level here.)

Although the focus of the see returned to Wells in the late 12th century, and for a brief period even the huge abbey of Glastonbury was joined to it, the diocese was officially declared a joint see of Bath and Wells in 1245. It has retained this title to the present day, although the church at Bath reverted to parochial status after the Reformation.

A vision of the future

In 1495 Bishop Oliver King, a close friend and adviser to Henry VII, moved from Exeter to become bishop of Bath and Wells. On a visit to Bath in 1499, he was shocked at the state of the priory church (as Bath Abbey was then called), and, after having a vision of the Trinity and angels ascending and descending ladders to and from Heaven, he determined to rebuild it. The bishop's vision is depicted on the west front of the building. He died in 1503, but the prior he appointed, William Birde, carried on the work, putting up the whole shell of the present building, with new, smaller transepts, over the next 25 years. Birde employed Robert and William Vertue, two of the greatest royal master masons of the time (though Robert died in 1506), as his designers, and the pair erected a rectangular tower over the new crossing, and put remarkable fan vaults into the chancel and even more elaborate pendant vaults into the chancel aisles. The other vaults were not completed until later – Sir George Gilbert Scott finally inserted the nave vault in 1869 – but the new church was clearly in use by the monks in the 1530s, just before the Dissolution. Prior Birde built himself a beautiful chantry chapel on the south side of the chancel, just before his death in 1525. Regrettably the church was left to decay following the dissolution of the monastery in 1539, and the nave had its roof removed. In the late 16th century, however, it became the parish church for Bath, and services resumed in the choir in 1576. Early in the 17th century, Bishop James Montague (1608–15) paid for the nave to be reroofed, and though he moved on to become bishop of Winchester, his body was brought back to Bath for burial, beneath a suitably fine monument in the nave.

RIGHT: Bishop Oliver King's new west front of the early 1500s features climbing ladders to heaven on the stair turrets. The Roman baths and pump room lie just to the south-west.

CARLISLE

CUMBRIA

DEDICATION

- Cathedral Church of the Holy and Undivided Trinity

HISTORY

- Roman fort, just south of Hadrian's Wall, acquires a church in the late 7th century
- Castle and new town built from 1092 under William II
- New Augustinian priory and church built from 1123
- New diocese created, with the bishop's seat here, from 1133
- Large new choir and presbytery built in the 13th and early 14th centuries
- Augustinian priory rebuilt c. 1470–1528
- Nave demolished in Commonwealth c. 1649–52
- Restoration under Dean Tait 1853–6

OF SPECIAL INTEREST

- Norman east end of nave and south transept
- Fifteenth-century choir stalls and carved misericords
- Fine late 15th- and early 16th-century carved wooden screen fragments
- Priory buildings, including the vaulted fratry (now a library above a refreshment room) and prior's house and tower with wonderful painted ceiling

ABOVE: Early 12th-century pillars at the east end of the nave flank the Border Regiment chapel of 1949, where, in the 12th century, the canons' stalls were situated.

RIGHT: This view of the cathedral from the south-west clearly illustrates the building's early 12th-century architecture. The east end of an earlier nave can be seen on the left; the rest of the nave was demolished c. 1649. On the extreme right a fragment of the chapter house entrance is visible. In times past, the canons' cloister would have occupied the foreground.

arlisle was the last medieval diocese to be created in England. In 1092 King William Rufus captured what was later to be the county of Cumberland from the Scots, and built a new castle and town at Carlisle. There was already an ancient church there, perhaps on the site of St Cuthbert's church, and in 1123 a new large monastic church was started for the Augustinian canons, under their prior, Athelwold. Ten years after this, a new diocese was created in the extreme north-west corner of England – earlier the area had been claimed by Glasgow diocese – and Athelwold became the first bishop. At this time the archbishop of Canterbury, William de Corbeil (1123–36), was also an Augustinian canon and papal legate, and the order was at its peak of popularity. Henry I also used the order to stabilize the borders, and new Augustinian houses were founded nearby at Lanercost and Hexham.

Lamentably five of the eight bays of the 12th-century nave of Carlisle Cathedral were demolished in the Commonwealth period (c. 1649). All that can be seen today of the original cathedral are the two eastern bays of the nave (now the Border Regiment Chapel), the south transept and the lower part of the crossing. Despite this, and some heavy 19th-century restoration, there is still some fine early 12th-century architecture in the cathedral.

An era of excellence

After Bishop Athelwold's death in 1155, no further bishops were appointed until the early 13th century. Then in 1218, Hugh, the Cistercian abbot of Beaulieu, was appointed bishop, and he started work

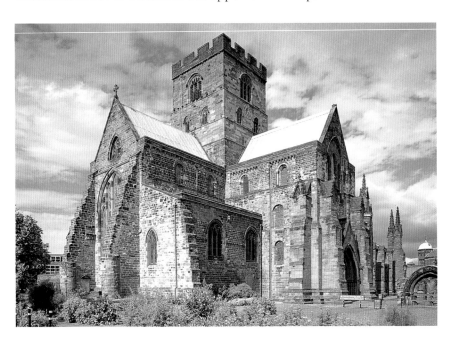

ABOVE: The early 14th-century great east window, with medieval glass in the top lights. The baldacchino over the high altar was designed by Sir Charles Nicholson (1867–1949) and gilded just after the Second World War by Stephen Dykes Bower.

ABOVE RIGHT: The spectacular eastern-arm ceiling was created in 1856 by the Victorian architect–designer Owen Jones, and repainted in 1970.

on a magnificent new eastern arm containing the choir and presbytery. The work seems to have been protracted, and sadly a fire gutted the new building in 1292. The stone-vaulted choir aisles survived, however, and in the early 14th century an even more splendid eastern arm was created with a really fabulous east window of nine lights and with tracery in the latest Decorated style. Luckily this was at a time when Carlisle was the base for Edward I's invasion of Scotland, and a parliament was held in the cathedral in 1307 with most of the court, including the archbishop of York and 19 bishops, attending. This brought the cathedral immense prestige. The great east window was finished and glazed just before the mid-14th century, and remarkably the top third of the original magnificent stained glass survives.

It was clearly the intention of the bishops and the priory that the nave should also be rebuilt, but unfortunately in 1380 the 12th-century crossing tower fell northwards in a severe storm onto the north transept, and a new two-storeyed tower and north transept had to be built first (the tower also had a small spire, which was removed in 1665). This new work was done by Bishop Strickland in the early 15th century, and about this time fine new stalls with carved misericords were put in the choir; the canopies were added later. Other small-scale works were carried out in the later 15th century, but the rebuilding of the nave never took place. The very fine early Renaissance Salkeld Screen was made for Lancelot Salkeld, the last prior, who became the first dean in 1542, after the dissolution of the Augustinian priory.

MEDIEVAL SECULAR

There were nine secular cathedrals in medieval England, but the largest of these, the old St Paul's, was destroyed by the Great Fire of London. Each cathedral was served by four 'principal persons' – Dean, Precentor, Chancellor and Treasurer – who sat at the four corners of the choir. There was also a large body of canons, each of whom had a prebend – an estate that gave the canon an income. Each canon had a deputy, called a vicar, who in the later Middle Ages attended almost all of the services on behalf of the canon, who was often absent. In the choir the canons occupied the back stalls, in front of which were the vicars' stalls, while the choristers' benches were in front again. Many of these cathedrals still contain the medieval stalls with tip-up seats, known as misericords. In the 'close' around the cathedral (usually a walled area with gates) were the canons' houses and the bishop's palace. There was usually an inner vicars' close, with its own hall and chapel, for the vicars – young men who lived communally and needed to be kept away from the temptations of the town. Most of these cathedrals also had fine chapter houses, which were often polygonal in plan, where the canons could meet.

ABOVE: Painting of Henry VI by Lambert Barnard (c. 1520), in Chichester Cathedral.
RIGHT: The great wooden vault below York Minster's central tower of c. 1470 is now one of the few original vaults in the cathedral. The central boss of saints Peter and Paul is five feet in diameter.

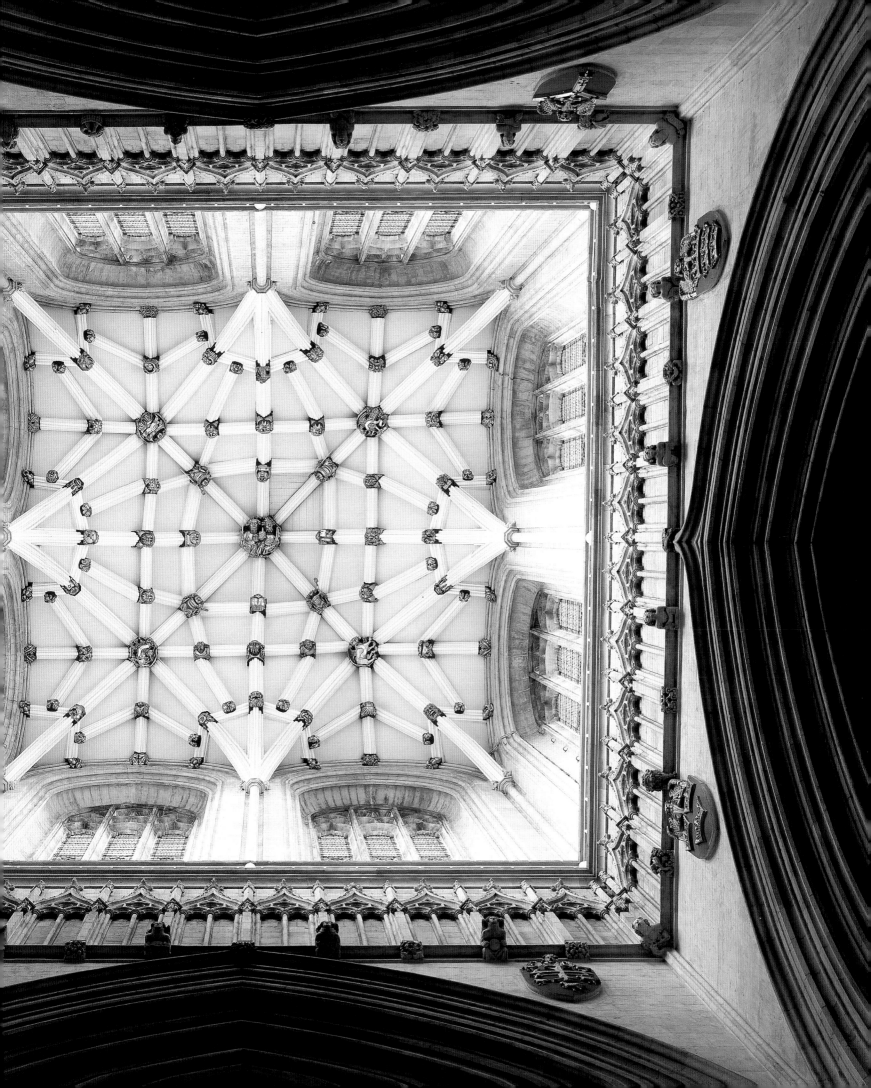

YORK MINSTER

NORTH YORKSHIRE

DEDICATION

• Cathedral Church of St Peter

HISTORY

• Paulinus is Bishop of York
  AD 627–33

• New Norman cathedral built
  c. 1080–1100

• Present cathedral built in many
  stages from c. 1220 to 1472

• Archbishop William Fitzherbert
  (d. 1154) canonized in 1227

• Archbishop Richard Scrope
  executed in 1405

• Cardinal Wolsey, archbishop
  1514–30

• Choir vault (1829) and nave vault
  (1840) both destroyed by fire

• Crossing area underpinned, 1967–
  1972, and 'crypt' museum created

• South transept vault burnt after a
  lightning strike in 1984

OF SPECIAL INTEREST

• Roman walls and 12th-century
  piers in 'crypt' museum

• Large quantities of fine medieval
  stained glass

• Tomb of Archbishop de Gray
  (d. 1255) in south transept

• Late 13th-century chapter house,
  containing 237 carved heads

• Very fine early 14th-century
  cupboards in Zouche chapel

• Many excellent archiepiscopal
  tombs

• Great choir screen (c. 1460)

• Fine marble paving (1730–36)

ABOVE: This screen at the entrance to the choir was made to house the carvings of all the kings of England, from William I to Henry VI.

RIGHT: The astronomical clock on the east side of the early 13th-century north transept was made in 1750 by Henry Hindley using 16th-century striking men-at-arms figures. On the left is the entrance to the chapter house vestibule.

ork Minster is today the largest Gothic cathedral in Britain, though before the Great Fire of 1666 it was exceeded in size by old St Paul's Cathedral in London. The total length of York Minster is 524 feet, and the height and width of its various spaces is very large indeed, making the volume of the nave, transepts and eastern arm – all of which have double aisles – huge. The disadvantage of this great size is that all of the vaults over these spaces had to be made in timber, not stone, and tragically most of the vaults, and the roofs above them, have been destroyed by fire in the last century and a half. The south transept vault and roof were burnt out as recently as 1984. Another problem at York has been the instability of the foundations, particularly in the crossing area, though this was finally resolved by a massive underpinning operation which took place from 1967 to 1972, accompanied by archaeological excavations. The result of the excavations is that a great deal more is now known of the early history of the site and buildings. Many of these recent archaeological discoveries are displayed in a new 'crypt' under the crossing area.

History reveals itself

York was one of the few places in Britain known to have sent a bishop to the late Roman Council of Arles in AD 314, but apart from this nothing is known of the bishop or his church. At this time York was one of the most important legionary fortresses in Britain, indeed in the north-west Roman Empire, and the remains of the fortress's headquarters can be seen below the crossing. The fortress was abandoned in the early 5th century AD, and Christianity did not return until 627 when Paulinus was sent from Kent to be the first new bishop of York. Despite the recent archaeological excavations, nothing has yet been found of the Anglo-Saxon cathedral in the city, and it was only after the Norman Conquest, and the appointment of Thomas of Bayeux as archbishop in 1070, that a new cathedral was started. Quite a lot is known about the Norman construction, thanks to the excavations. It was a large, but most unusual, building: 361 feet long with a 45-foot-wide nave without aisles. There were also large unaisled transepts with eastern apses, and a long chancel also with an eastern apse. This building was probably complete by the time of Archbishop Thomas's death in 1100, and over the next two centuries almost all of the Norman cathedral was replaced by new, larger Gothic structures. There are still, however, a few fragments of the Norman cathedral above the vaults in the area around the crossing tower.

The first major addition to the Norman cathedral came in about 1160, when a wonderful new eastern arm was built in the highest quality ashlar masonry (with Magnesian limestone), and with superb carved late Romanesque decoration. It had small eastern transepts, and was almost certainly trying to be even more splendid than the

ABOVE: A new statue of the Roman emperor Constantine has been erected outside the south transept.

RIGHT: These remnants of Romanesque piers in the crypt are all that remains of the magnificent eastern arm of the early 12th-century cathedral, which, like Durham, must have had many incised piers.

magnificent new early 12th-century eastern arm at Canterbury. Sadly, this structure was demolished in the late 14th century, and all that remains today are some of its beautiful carved piers in the crypt, which were uncovered again in 1829. These fragments, which have echoes of the mid-12th-century work in Durham and Canterbury, give a flavour of what the choir above was like.

The 13th century
The next stage of the rebuilding work, and the first stage to survive intact to the present day, was in the great transepts in the early 13th century. This work was also to a certain extent trying to compete with Canterbury, and in particular with the popularity of the new shrine of St Thomas Becket. In 1227 a former archbishop of York, William Fitzherbert, was canonized by the Pope, and his first shrine was at the east end of the nave. The south transept would, therefore, make a grand new entrance for the pilgrims coming to the shrine, and the patron of the new work was the archbishop,

Walter de Gray (1215–55), who also had his own chantry chapel built in the central eastern chapel of the south transept. When de Gray died he was buried here, and his magnificent Purbeck marble tomb survives to this day. When the tomb was opened in 1968, the coffin was still intact with a unique painted portrait of the archbishop on the wooden lid, and inside were the archbishop's crozier, chalice, paten and ring. The north transept was rebuilt at about the same time as the south transept, but it has many features in it that are different: the most famous of these is the exceptionally tall five-light north window. The five lancets of equal height, here known as the 'five sisters', are 53 feet high but only five feet wide. They still contain much of their original grisaille glass, which was installed in about 1250 when the construction work was complete. The last stage of the work here was the building of a new crossing tower with a timber and lead spire on top. This was probably well over 300 feet high, but unfortunately it collapsed in 1407.

In the middle of the 13th century, Westminster Abbey and Salisbury Cathedral were in the process of putting up fine new octagonal chapter houses with large traceried windows. York followed soon afterwards with an even grander octagonal chapter house without a central pillar. It has a wooden vault (with a 58 foot span), and here the original timber roof above still survives, one of the finest and most complex examples of medieval carpentry in Britain. Unlike Salisbury, York

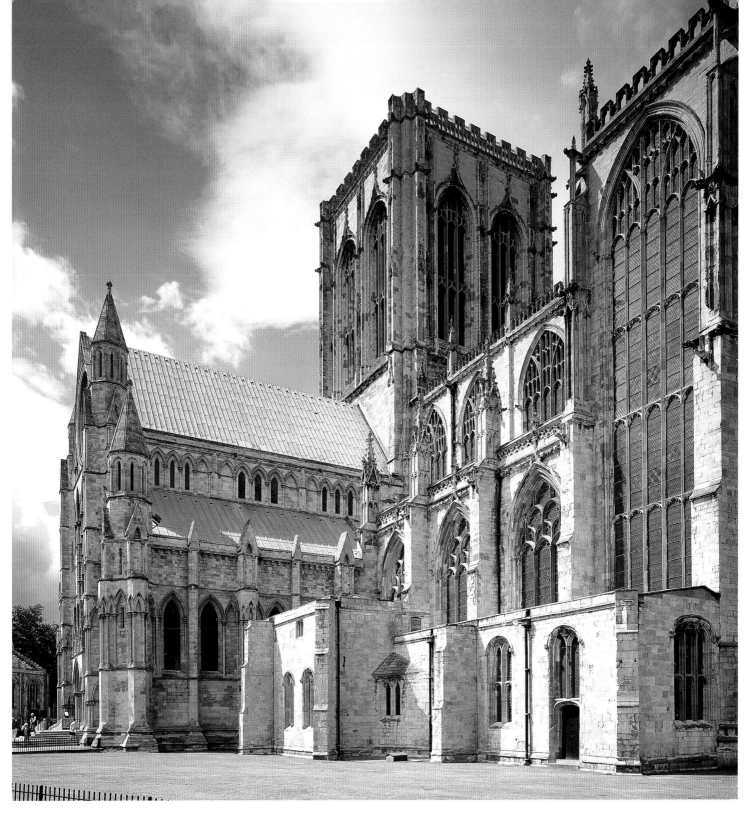

ABOVE: The Minster as seen
from the south-east, with
the 13th-century south
transept on the left. In
the foreground is the early
14th-century Zouche chapel
with, towering above it, the
great St Cuthbert window
(glazed c. 1440) in the
south-east transept.

never built a large cloister, though the
L-shaped passage from the north transept is
an exceptionally grand affair.

Rebuilding the nave

By the 1290s the chapter house was complete,
and work started on the rebuilding of the nave.
Large new foundations were dug outside the
old nave walls, about 100 feet apart, making
this by far the widest nave in England, and in
1291 Archbishop Romeyn laid the first stone at

the east end of the southern foundation. When
the old nave walls were demolished, their
foundations were used for the very large new
arcades. At the beginning of Edward I's
Scottish Wars in 1297, York became the
administrative centre of England, with parlia-
ments being held in the chapter house. The
rebuilding of the nave became an even more
prestigious project, and in the early 14th century it was modified to include large new western towers and a new west front. By this time,

the stone vaults of the aisles were going in, and it was intended to make the high vault in stone as well. This never happened, and after the Black Death a wooden vault was installed instead. By the 1330s the great west window, with its curvilinear tracery, was being inserted, but the western towers were only reaching their second stage. After a long break, the southern tower was finally completed in 1433–46 (when it became the belfry), while the northern tower was not finished until the late 15th century.

Despite the Black Death, and the non-completion of the nave, yet another very grand scheme for rebuilding the eastern arm was drawn up and started under Archbishop William de la Zouche (1342–52), and it seems as though timber vaults were planned for here from the beginning. This work was carried out in two main stages. First came the Lady chapel in the eastern four bays, the side walls of which were built rapidly between 1361 and 1373. Then there was a pause of two decades before the western part – the choir and presbytery – was rebuilt between 1395 and 1405. By the latter date all the main work was finished, and in October 1405 an agreement was drawn up to glaze the great east window. This enormous window, 74 feet high by 32 feet wide, still contains this glazing, the largest area of medieval painted glass surviving anywhere in Europe. At just about the time that the glazing was being completed in 1407, another major disaster happened: the masonry of the upper part of the central tower collapsed.

Following this, King Henry IV sent his own master mason from Westminster to supervise the building of a new tower and the strengthening of the piers. The first part of the work progressed well, but it seems clear that the building of a great two-stage tower would never be achieved because of the instability of the foundations. This problem was in fact only remedied in 1972, 500 years after the final work was completed. The lantern is over 200 feet high, but in proportion to the rest of the great church it is too low, unlike the great crossing tower at Canterbury. Despite this, York Minster is a stupendous achievement, and one of the largest buildings ever to be erected in medieval Europe.

LEFT: The remarkable painted timber vault over the chapter house is suspended from a contemporary roof, and it is one of the most complex medieval carpentry structures in Europe.

LINCOLN MINSTER

LINCOLNSHIRE

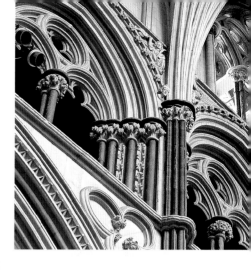

ABOVE RIGHT: The upper spandrels of the Angel Choir at the east end of the Minster are filled with beautifully carved angels.

BELOW: The grand towers of Lincoln Minster dominate the repetitive tiled roofs of the local houses.

incoln Minster is perhaps the most spectacular of all the great Gothic cathedrals in England. Its hilltop site, when viewed from the south, makes it stand out like none other, not even Durham. In the late Middle Ages the three great towers were capped by timber and lead spires, with the central tower's spire rising to over 450 feet. Sadly this spire was destroyed in 1548, though the western spires survived until 1807.

Ancient origins

The first cathedral in Lincoln, a major Roman city, may have been built for a late Roman bishop, but there is a tantalizing reference in Bede's *Ecclesiastical History* to the building of a stone church there in AD 628–9, which may have been for an early Anglo-Saxon bishop appointed by Bishop Paulinus of York. In 1978–9 excavations in the centre of the Roman city, on the site of the church of St Paul-in-the-Bail, found traces of a very early church, with an apsidal east end, at the centre of the Roman forum. This may have been the early church, but all of this was destroyed by the Vikings.

At the time of the Norman Conquest there was a vast diocese, with its cathedral at Dorchester-upon-Thames, which stretched all the way

from the Thames to the Humber on the north side of Lincolnshire. William the Conqueror established a new castle in the upper part of the walled Roman city, and in 1072 the new Norman bishop of Dorchester, Remigius, was instructed by the king (with the Pope's and archbishop of Canterbury's agreement) to move his cathedral to a new site just to the east of Lincoln Castle. Here he built a new cathedral, which seems in part to have been based on Archbishop Lanfranc's cathedral in Canterbury. It had an eastern apse, just inside the eastern city wall of Lincoln, and relatively small transepts. There was, however, a long nave and a large west front, which made the new cathedral over 300 feet long. The work was finished by the time of Remigius's death in 1092, and over the next half century or so there were various changes to the building, including the addition of two western towers. Today only the original west front and the lower parts of the western towers survive, because the whole of the rest of the building was replaced by the stupendous Gothic cathedral that survives to this day. It is one of the finest and most beautiful cathedrals in western Europe, and it was constructed in less than a century (c. 1192–1280).

A natural disaster

The starting point for this new work was an earthquake, which took place on 15 April 1185, and was said to have 'split the minster from top to bottom'. This 'earthquake' may only have caused the collapse of the central tower, but it gave the new bishop, Hugh of Avalon, who was appointed the following year, a huge task to raise the money for the rebuilding. Hugh was a Carthusian monk from Witham Priory in Somerset, and it seems likely that he had seen the remarkable rebuilding of the choir at Canterbury in the 10 years following the fire of 1174. He therefore set about his task at Lincoln with alacrity. Over the next 15 years, until his death in 1200, Hugh erected an

ABOVE LEFT: At the far end of the magnificent early 13th-century nave is an early 14th-century choir screen topped by a fine 'Father Willis' organ (Willis was England's greatest 19th-century organ builder).

LEFT: The unusual arcading in the south choir aisle may have been inspired by the Trinity chapel in Canterbury Cathedral.

RIGHT: The 'crazy vaults' over the choir are, most unusually, asymmetric and have a rather syncopated feel to them.

ABOVE: The high altar in the Angel Choir has a stone canopy in Gothic style, designed by James Essex in 1769. On the left is the finely sculpted Easter sepulchre.

were finished. However, the extraordinary high vaults, which are sometimes called the 'crazy vaults', and the timber roofs above (large sections of which survive, and have been dated by tree-ring dating), were not finished for perhaps another decade, by which time King John had brought chaos to England.

The impetus of Bishop Hugh

In 1220, the year in which the shrine of St Thomas Becket in Canterbury was completed, Bishop Hugh of Avalon was canonized by the Pope. This led to a remarkable new surge of building work that rivalled even the work on the new cathedral at Salisbury. A huge new nave was built, with some extra chapels outside it on the north-west and south-west. At the same time the great transepts were completed and, again as at Salisbury, a huge new west façade for imagery, with large outer stair-turrets, was started. This flanks and spreads over the top of the Romanesque west front. In about 1238 the crossing tower seems to have fallen, but this led immediately to its rebuilding with a large new lantern above. By about 1250 this rebuilding work, and the work to finish the high gable to the west front, were complete, but this was not all that was happening. A magnificent new Galilee porch was added to the west side of the south transept, and a beautiful new 10-sided chapter house was built on the north-east, with a vestibule and what was probably intended to be the start of a large new northern cloister. Just after all of this was completed, under the great bishop, Robert Grosseteste (1235–53), a completely new scheme was started to replace and greatly extend the east end of the cathedral, which had been built only half a century before. This was, no doubt, inspired by the new 'French' architecture of Westminster Abbey, and was undertaken to provide a more magnificent setting for the shrine of St Hugh, as demanded

extraordinary new eastern arm (now called St Hugh's choir) which gave the cathedral double transepts, each with a series of eastern chapels, and a remarkable polygonal east end, with stair turrets on either side. This echoes the corona of Canterbury Cathedral. To build this new east end the Roman city wall had to be demolished, and this also led to the building of a new eastern city wall. By the time of Bishop Hugh's death, the main walls of the new eastern arm by the papal bull of canonization. The plan of the new east end followed that of the recently completed new east end for Ely Cathedral. It allowed the new high altar and shrine for St Hugh to be built on the site of the old eastern chapel, but surrounded by the magnificent architecture of what is now known as the 'Angel Choir'. This superb space, which completes the Gothic architecture of the cathedral, was laid out in 1256 once permission had been given to demolish the city wall yet again.

Completion

The cathedral now had a total length of 482 feet, and more than 20 years were needed to complete the whole structure, which was filled with the new early Geometric tracery and carved angels as are found in Westminster Abbey. At the abbey, the shrine of St Edward was finally completed for Henry III in 1269. A decade afterwards, on 6 October 1280, King Edward I and Queen Eleanor of Castile came to Lincoln, accompanied by the archbishop of Canterbury and many others, to see the wonderful new shrine of St Hugh consecrated. The shrine survived until 1542, when all traces of it were removed by Henry VIII. With the completion of the Angel Choir, the cathedral as a great Gothic space was finished. The extraordinary task of heightening the crossing tower to 270 feet, however, continued in the early years of the 14th century. Then on top of this was placed a colossal timber and lead spire (blown down in 1548, as we have already seen), which was itself perhaps 200 feet high, making the whole structure reach to well over 450 feet above the ground. It may even have been as much as 481 feet high, which was the total internal length of the cathedral – and also by chance the height of the Great Pyramid in Egypt. The dean of Lincoln at the time of the completion of the tower and spire was a man called Roger Martival. In 1315 Martival became bishop of Salisbury, and he was almost certainly the man who helped complete Salisbury's extraordinary tower and stone spire. By the early 15th century the twin western towers of Lincoln were heightened to 206 feet and given their own spires, providing the cathedral with its unsurpassed verticality.

RIGHT: At the centre of the western façade are three great early Norman arches, resembling a Roman triumphal arch. The large 13th-century screen wall was built to hold hundreds of statues.

SALISBURY

WILTSHIRE

ABOVE: These medieval
paintings on the choir
vault were restored in
the late 19th century.

RIGHT: The west front
is newly cleaned
and repaired; sadly
such conservation is
hugely expensive.

BELOW: The southern
choir stalls were first
made for the canons
and vicars in 1236.

alisbury Cathedral was the only completely new cathedral to be erected in England in the later Middle Ages. It is an immense structure about 460 feet long, built – minus its great tower and spire – in less than 40 years on a new site in the first half of the 13th century.

Origins of a great cathedral

Before looking at the building's history in more detail, its origins should first be considered. In the late Anglo-Saxon period the diocese for Wiltshire and Berkshire was based at Ramsbury, and in 1058 this was joined to the diocese for Dorset, based at the Benedictine abbey at Sherborne. Then, after the Norman Conquest, the see was transferred to Old Sarum (as it is now called), a large Iron Age hill fort, within which a Norman castle had been built. Here a new, quite small, cathedral was built between 1075 and 1092. In the early 12th century this was greatly enlarged to the east with double-aisled transepts and a new choir and presbytery. During this time the cathedral was enlarging its estates and establishment, and by the later 12th century there was a cloister and a large bishop's residence to the north. The hilltop site was both cramped and very exposed, and before the end of the 12th century a decision was taken to move down to a completely new site, beside the River Avon, two miles to the south. The move did not actually take place until after the end of King John's chaotic reign, but by 1218 the Pope had given his permission and work began on laying out not only a large new cathedral close but also a new town at Salisbury.

Work started on the cathedral itself in 1220, and from the beginning was on a very large and ambitious scale. The plan of the whole building was marked out on the ground, and five-foot-deep foundations were dug down to the natural river gravel. Then work started on the three eastern chapels, with the central one being given remarkable aisles, separated off by arcades with long and slender shafts of Purbeck marble. As the whole cathedral was dedicated to the Virgin Mary, this was the Trinity chapel. It was, however, hoped that the chapel would hold a new shrine for Bishop Osmund (1078–99), whose canonization was being actively sought from the Pope. The three eastern chapels were ready by 1225, and the altars were consecrated. The following year the first burial (of the Earl of Salisbury) took place

ABOVE: Fourteenth-century strainer arches in the eastern crossing are confusing to the eye at first glance, but intriguing. Beneath lie the presbytery and high altar area. The tombs that are visible on either side of the presbytery are those of the two bishops who built the tower and spire: Simon of Ghent and Roger Martival.

here, and the bodies of three great Norman bishops, Osmund, Roger and Jocelin, were brought from Old Sarum. Remarkably, the 12th-century marble covers for the coffins still survive in the cathedral.

Work then continued rapidly on building the whole eastern arm of the cathedral, which was achieved in about 10 years (1226–36), despite the fact that the high vault, at 84 feet, was the tallest yet built in England. (Two decades later an even higher vault was built at Westminster Abbey.) Salisbury's eastern arm was on a very large scale, with double transepts that overall contained 10 additional altars, and a very long choir and presbytery. The quality of the ashlar masonry is quite exceptional. In addition, a huge quantity of Purbeck marble was used – much more than in any other cathedral in England – for capitals, columns, bases and string-courses, as well as for the column

drums and some decoration. Once the masonry of the eastern arm was completed, coloured glass was put in the many large lancet windows, and much of the plain walling and vaulting was covered in painted decoration. In June 1236 King Henry III gave 20 'good oaks' from his forest at Chippenham to the dean and canons 'to make stalls in their church'. This must indicate that the roof and vaults were complete by this time, and the furnishing work could be started. Remarkably these stalls, all 106 of them, still survive in the cathedral, the largest and earliest complete set in England. By this time Salisbury had 52 canons, and each had a deputy, or 'vicar', who occupied the stall in front. By 1245 the eastern arm and choir were in full use, and work was continuing on the 10-bay nave (200 feet long), the north porch and the west front. The windows of the nave were all given much coloured glass (almost all of it sadly destroyed in 1790), but there is no evidence of painted decoration here, only the whitewashing of the walls and the covering of this with red lines. The vaulted north porch was built to be the principal entrance to the cathedral, as at many other cathedrals, and it, too, is exceptionally large. Above the principal entrance is a beautiful little room, known as the parvise chamber, which has its own separate miniature staircase. This chamber is still covered by its original timber roof, the finest in the cathedral. The north-facing windows, with window seats, originally looked directly onto the great cathedral bell-tower. This wonderful early 13th-century structure, which was topped by a timber and lead spire over 200 feet high, was knocked down in the 18th century.

The west front of the cathedral is a great stone façade, about 110-foot square, which terminates in large outer stair turrets, capped by spirelets and a high gable. This great screen wall was built up in layers as the nave was built, and it was made to contain a mass of sculpture in shallow niches. Unlike at Wells Cathedral, however, only the buttress faces and the lowest tiers were ever used, and most of the sculpture in place today dates from the later 19th century. By 1258 the cathedral was finished, after only 38 years, and a great consecration ceremony took place on 30 September.

Changing styles

The whole of Salisbury Cathedral is built in a uniform early Gothic style with lancet windows

ABOVE: The eastern Trinity chapel is an interesting blend of slender ancient Purbeck marble shafts and modern French stained glass, designed and installed by Gabriel Loire of Chartres in 1980.

(a few quatrefoil windows are also used). However, a completely new French Gothic style was introduced at Westminster Abbey from 1246, and soon afterwards this, with traceried windows, was being used in the octagonal chapter house and cloister at Salisbury. The cloister had been planned from the beginning, but in the middle of the 13th century it was decided to enlarge it on the west and south, to make it the biggest cloister in England. At the same time it was decided to use the new tracery in the windows of the cloister arcades (with glass in iron frames in the upper lights), and to widen the cloister walks and cover them with stone vaults. All this work was probably finished by the late 1260s, giving Salisbury in only half a century not only a magnificent cathedral but also a very large cloister, chapter house and free-standing bell-tower. One thing was still missing, however: the enormous stone tower and spire.

Reaching for the heavens

Work on this great afterthought probably got under way at the very beginning of the 14th century, at a time when other cathedrals, like Ely, were also experimenting with daring new structures. A structure of this height (the top of the spire is over 400 feet above the ground, and the spire alone is 180 feet high) was, of course, not contemplated in the early 13th century. Some very tall timber and lead spires, similar to those at Old St Paul's and Lincoln, were being erected, and Salisbury's great stone spire was a culmination of this trend. The original cathedral had only a low lantern tower over the crossing. When work started on the new tower, a boarded timber ceiling was put over the crossing (the stone vault over the crossing was made only in 1479) and the top of the old tower was bound up with a series of huge wrought-iron bars – the largest medieval iron bars in

RIGHT: The nave looking east to the high altar and Trinity chapel. Until the 1870s there was always a stone screen at the crossing in front of the high altar. This was replaced with a Victorian ironwork screen, which was removed and destroyed in 1960. The complex lierne vault over the crossing was installed in 1479–80.

ABOVE: This detail of the triforium shows off the dark Purbeck marble shafts and capitals that support the deeply moulded early 13th-century Tisbury stone arcading.

England. A large two-storeyed tower was then constructed, and it was covered externally in a mass of fine Decorated-style panelling and gables. Above, thousands of individually carved ballflowers were made on the string-courses, mullions and jambs. This decoration was very costly. At the top of the tower, arches (called squinches) were made across the diagonals to support the octagonal spire, and a new internal timber scaffold was made to build the spire from the inside outwards. Pairs of pinnacles, also all covered in ballflower, were put on each of the corners of the tower to give weight to the base of the spire, and then the remarkably thin shell of the spire was rapidly built. Each block in the spire is joined to its neighbour by iron cramps set in lead. Once the upper part of the spire had been reached an external door was made in the north face. This allowed access to a small external scaffold for the very top of the spire and the capstone. Running vertically through the capstone to the cross was an iron bar that was attached to the top of the internal timber frame. Because of this the medieval scaffolding in the spire has never been removed, only added to.

EXETER

DEVON

ABOVE RIGHT: The south-east view of the cathedral shows the Lady chapel on the right and the bishop's palace and private chapel in the foreground.

xeter Cathedral is most famous today for its wonderful high vault, which continues unbroken for over 300 feet above the nave, choir and presbytery. It is a tierceron vault of exceptional splendour, and the view of it from inside the west doorway is particularly fine.

In the later Anglo-Saxon period the cathedral for Devon was situated at Crediton, and to this was added the diocese for Cornwall in about 1027. Then, in 1050, King Edward the Confessor came to Devon, and moved the cathedral from Crediton to the church of St Peter in Exeter, where he installed Leofric as its first bishop. Foundations of this late Anglo-Saxon cathedral were excavated on the site of the Victorian church of St Mary Major, just to the west of the present cathedral, in 1971. After the Conquest the first Norman bishop, Osbern (1072–1103) does not seem to have rebuilt his Anglo-Saxon church – most unusually – and it was left to his successor, William Warelwast (1107–37), a nephew of William the Conqueror, to start the building of the present cathedral in about 1112. Today only small fragments of the lower walls of the nave and choir of this early 12th-century church survive, as well as the magnificent flanking towers, which became the principal transepts in the 14th century. These towers still display externally much of their early 12th-century Romanesque decoration of blind arcading and carved chevrons.

BELOW: Half-way down the nave is a modern altar for Sunday morning Eucharist, while the minstrels' gallery is high up on the right.

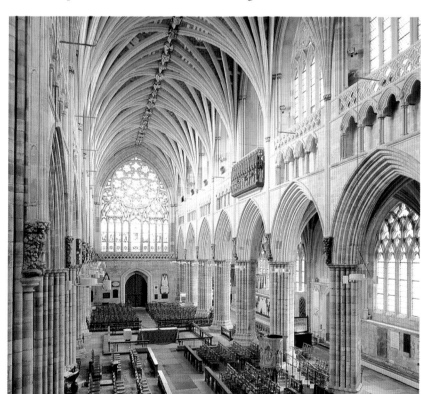

DEDICATION

• Cathedral Church of St Peter

HISTORY

• Diocese created in 1050, and first cathedral of St Mary in use from 1050 to *c.* 1120

• New late Norman cathedral built 1112–*c.* 1200

• Dean appointed and chapter house built in 1225

• Cathedral completely rebuilt *c.* 1275–1375

• Upper parts of towers rebuilt in the late 15th century

• Cathedral restored by Sir George Gilbert Scott 1870–77

• South-east side of the cathedral blitzed in May 1942

OF SPECIAL INTEREST

• Choir stalls and bishop's throne (early 14th century) and some early 13th-century misericords

• Tierceron vaults and carved and painted bosses

• Image screen outside west front with many fine statues

• Medieval bishop's palace and canons' houses around the cathedral

ABOVE: Floodlit view of the cathedral from the north-west. The lowest part of the west front's sculpture screen was made *c.* 1340, with an upper row of statues added in the 15th century.

A late starter

Throughout the Middle Ages this cathedral seems to have done everything later than all the other English cathedrals to the north-east. Not only was it very late in starting its Norman rebuilding, but this was not finally finished until about 1200. Moreover, it was only in 1225 that the first dean was appointed. This led on quickly to the building of the first chapter house – a rectangular building that still survives to the south of the south transept – the meeting place for the new dean and the 24 canons. Most other cathedrals were hard at work during the 13th century rebuilding their eastern arms on a much larger scale, but at Exeter this work did not start until the 1270s, when Bishop Walter Branscombe (1258–80) started to build the fine new eastern arm, with a plan clearly based on that of Salisbury. In the centre of the east end was a fine Lady chapel, and it was here that the

wonderful sequence of tierceron vaults was started. Tiercerons are the secondary ribs running from the springing point to the carved bosses on the ridge rib. From 1279 onwards, Exeter has an almost complete set of fabric accounts which, uniquely, allows us both to understand and to date precisely most stages of the rebuilding work over the next 90 years. The accounts also tell us much about the material used and where it came from. For example, Purbeck marble came from Corfe; the wonderful carved bosses along the ridge-ribs, initially in the presbytery, were made originally from Ham Hill stone (from south Somerset); later, Portland stone and Caen stone from Normandy were chosen; while in the nave there is only the local Beer stone. Each of the Ham Hill stone bosses cost 5 shillings (25p).

From about 1298 the bishop, dean and canons agreed that they would all contribute

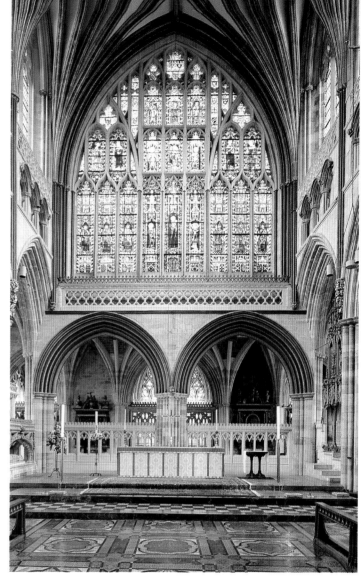

ABOVE: The choir looking west with the tierceron vaults above, and the very fine canopied stalls in the foreground. The dean sits in the stall to the left of the doorway with the precentor on the right.

ABOVE RIGHT: The great east window, which sits above the high altar, was built in the early 14th century, but received new Perpendicular tracery and stained glass in 1390.

large fixed sums from their own annual incomes, to allow the rebuilding work to continue rapidly. In 1308 King Edward II's treasurer, Walter Stapledon, became bishop, and because he had become very rich he agreed to give very large sums. In 1325 he increased his annual contribution to 1,000 marks (£666.66), a huge sum. Sadly Stapledon was murdered in London the very next year, not long before the king himself was murdered. In 1328 John Grandisson was made bishop, and he was likewise determined to provide a good deal of money to see the work to completion. By this time much of the eastern arm was finished, and the work had reached the first bay of the nave. Bishop Grandisson wrote to Pope John XXII, whose chaplain he had been: 'the cathedral of Exeter, now finished up to the nave, is marvellous in beauty and when completed will surpass every church of its kind in

England and France'. Luckily Grandisson lived until 1369, and despite the ravages of the Black Death he managed to see the great task almost to completion. He also started to add a very fine image screen to the outside of the west front, which still survives along with many of its beautiful statues. Into the back of this screen Grandisson made a tiny chantry chapel for himself, with the carved figure of the Trinity on the vault above looking down onto his tomb.

Work was halted for four years (1349–53) when the Black Death struck, and though 10 canons and many others in Exeter died, the bishop pushed on with the work. By the 1370s – a century after the rebuilding of the cathedral was started – it was finished, and the interior had become the wonderful setting for the liturgy that Grandisson wanted. Traces of this liturgy can still be seen in the very fine minstrels' gallery on the north side of the nave

ABOVE: The superb pulpitum screen, which was created between 1318 and 1325. The two openings to the choir stalls were cut through only in the 1870s.

BELOW: The minstrels' gallery, where a concealed choir or band of musicians performed, is still used today.

and in the wonderful carved screen between the nave and the choir. Within the choir itself are some excellent carved stalls, and the most splendid of all the bishop's thrones in England (see picture on page 10). The throne was completed in 1312 by master carpenter, Robert Gampton. Made of wood, it is a miniature work of architecture in its own right, as are the vaults in the two transepts. The Norman towers were left untouched externally, but inside they were given new wall-faces and high galleries. Timber tierceron vaults were added over the top of the galleries in 1321–2, which can be compared with the spectacular contemporary vaults in the octagon at Ely Cathedral.

By the end of the 14th century, Exeter cathedral had almost reached its present form. In 1389–90 the great nine-light east window was given new Perpendicular tracery. Elsewhere, however, the building still contains its wonderful sequence of Decorated-style window tracery, which changes and develops from east to west.

CHICHESTER

WEST SUSSEX

he original cathedral for the South Saxons was built by St Wilfrid on the island of Selsey in about 681. The site of the cathedral is probably beneath the partially demolished church at Church Norton on Selsey, and the story of it being washed away by the sea is a myth. The bishop's seat was moved from here to the old Roman walled city of Chichester in 1075. A new early Norman cathedral was started soon afterwards by Bishop Stigand (1070–87), and this had a semicircular ambulatory with semicircular chapels off it. The choir was situated under the crossing, and there were small transepts (also with small semicircular apses to the east) and an eight-bay nave. The western part of the nave, and the western towers, were probably not completed until the early 12th century.

A disastrous fire

On 20 October 1187 a fire completely gutted both the cathedral and the city. Soon afterwards rebuilding work was started in the old shell, and burnt masonry can still be seen. In the nave, fine new ashlar masonry and Purbeck marble shafting was installed, while in the eastern arm the semicircular ambulatory was demolished and replaced with a square east end and two new chapels. Some exceptionally fine

ABOVE RIGHT: The altar of St Richard is dominated by the 1985 tapestry by Ursula Benker-Schirmer.

BELOW: The Lady chapel, as enlarged in the early 14th century, with John Skelton's 1988 statue of the Virgin and Child on the left.

DEDICATION

• Cathedral Church of the Holy Trinity

HISTORY

• Diocese for Sussex created with cathedral at Selsey in AD 681
• New Norman cathedral built in Anglo-Saxon city of Chichester 1075–c. 1150
• Bishop Richard Wych (1245–53) canonized in 1262 and shrine built behind the high altar (destroyed in 1538)
• Major rebuilding works with new vaults and roofs c. 1275–1330
• Collapse of north-west tower in 1635 (rebuilt in 1901)
• Siege by parliamentary troops in 1642
• Collapse of tower and spire on 21 February 1861 – rebuilt by Sir George Gilbert Scott

OF SPECIAL INTEREST

• Two very fine early 12th-century carved panels in south choir aisle
• Fine choir stalls and misericords (c. 1330)
• Early 16th-century painted panels of bishops and kings in transepts
• Many good later 19th-century fittings and stained glass
• Remarkable collection of mid-20th-century works of art (many commissioned by Dean Hussey)
• Fine cloister, canons' houses, vicars' close, 'prebendal' school, bishop's palace and bell-tower

Purbeck marble composite Corinthian capitals were also put in on either side of what was later to become the site of the shrine of St Richard. During this work, stone vaults were put into the building for the first time. In the early 13th century new vaulted porches were added either side of the nave, and not long afterwards a new scheme was started to make a series of additional chapels outside the nave aisle walls. This was very common in France, but not in Britain, where Elgin Cathedral in Scotland is the only parallel.

As at Winchester, Chichester Cathedral is situated on a difficult, uneven site in the Roman city, and much settlement took place during and after the building works. In 1210 the south-west tower collapsed and was rebuilt, and the new 13th-century masonry is still visible, filling the cracks in the old Norman work. The crossing tower was given a new lantern in the mid-13th century, and this may have had a timber and lead spire on top.

A shrine to St Richard

In 1262 Bishop Richard Wych was canonized (he became St Richard of Chichester), and in 1276 his remains were translated to the cathedral's east end, behind the high altar. The site became an important shrine. Soon after this a small west porch was added to the nave; then all the upper clerestory walls, first of the nave and then of the presbytery, were altered and new roofs were put on. This work took place after the earlier walls had settled, and the magnificent nave and presbytery roof trusses still survive in situ above the vaults. The age of the trusses has recently been confirmed by tree-ring dating.

Once this work was done and a new rose window had been put in the high east gable, the 12th-century eastern Lady chapel was

completely rebuilt and extended two bays eastwards in the early 14th century, making this once comparatively small cathedral more than 400 feet long. New windows with Decorated tracery and fine tierceron vaults were also put in the Lady chapel, and the inside must then have been lavishly painted. By this time the south transept was being used as the chapter house, and its south wall, with a wonderful new seven-light traceried window, was completely rebuilt under Bishop Langton (1305–37). Beneath the window Langton installed his own fine canopied tomb; he also paid for a magnificent new set of choir stalls under the crossing.

In the 15th century the outer wall of the north transept was rebuilt, and another very large new window was put in, this time in the Perpendicular style. At about the same time a magnificent new stone spire was added to the top of the 13th-century crossing tower. This spire was clearly modelled on the huge early 14th-century spire at Salisbury, and it must have added much weight to the Romanesque crossing piers beneath. The spire survived for at least 450 years before its famous collapse on 21 February 1861. After this, as is well known, the spire was rebuilt in five years under Sir George Gilbert Scott, and though it was built as a replica of the earlier spire, the tower was heightened by six feet during the work, bringing the total height of the spire today to 277 feet.

In the later Middle Ages, only minor works were carried out at the cathedral, but in the surrounding close quite a lot of late medieval construction took place. On the south-east a fine new hall and separate close were built for the vicars, while several new houses were built for the canons and chantry priests, and a series of fine covered walkways were made south of the cathedral that now act as a sort of cloister. To the north of the nave, a magnificent new free-standing stone bell-tower was built, which is now a rarity in England. Finally, the bishop enlarged his fine residence to the south-west of the cathedral in the early Tudor period, adding fine new private chambers and a great brick wall round the court to the south.

RIGHT: The cathedral from the south-east, with the Lady chapel on the right. The Lady chapel returned to its medieval use only in 1871, after a century and a half as the cathedral library. The cathedral has copper roofs, which were a cheap alternative to lead in the mid-20th century.

71

LICHFIELD
STAFFORDSHIRE

ABOVE: The choir and high altar with its 19th-century iron screen. This wonderful example of high Victorian art is still in situ, unlike the great Victorian screens at Salisbury and Hereford.

BELOW: A whole series of restorations took place between the late 18th and late 19th centuries, which provided a fine set of Victorian furnishings, including this Minton tile floor.

ichfield Cathedral is the only medieval cathedral in England still to be crowned by three spires, all of them made of stone, with the central spire rising to 258 feet. The western towers are just under 200 feet high. The cathedral was, however, very badly damaged in the English Civil War, and so a great deal of the medieval masonry had to be rebuilt in 1661–9. The cathedral was also heavily restored in the later 19th century by Sir George Gilbert Scott and his son John Oldrid Scott, and it is only in recent years that the complicated architectural history of the eastern arm has been partly deciphered.

An auspicious start

The fifth of the bishops of Mercia, St Chad, fixed his abode and church at Stowe, a mile to the north-east of Lichfield, and died there in 672. Then in 700 Bishop Hedda consecrated a new church on the site of the present cathedral and brought to it St Chad's body. The church became an important cathedral in the late 8th century, when Mercia was the most powerful kingdom in England. From 787 to 803, under King Offa, it was the seat of the archbishopric of Lichfield, cut out of the province of Canterbury. This status did not endure, and by the time of the Norman Conquest, the cathedral was so poor that in 1075 the bishop's seat was moved to Chester. It moved on to Coventry in 1095, but at the same time a large new Norman church was being built at Lichfield. By the early 13th century it was once again a cathedral, with the diocese being called 'Coventry and Lichfield'. This was the time when the first part of the present cathedral was being erected, and the architecture around the choir dates from the early 13th century. Below the floors of the eastern arm, archaeology has revealed a whole series of foundations, which show that from the late 11th century to the late 12th century the eastern arm developed rapidly from a church with a semicircular ambulatory with apsidal chapels, to a large square-ended building with a Lady chapel and perhaps a new shrine for St Chad. It thus developed in a similar fashion to Chichester Cathedral.

From about 1200 work had started on a completely new cathedral that would progressively replace the old Romanesque one. As usual the eastern arm was the starting point, and by about 1240 the choir and both the transepts had been finished, as well as a remarkable new three-storeyed building on the south side of the choir, which housed in its upper level the chapel of St Chad's Head.

In 1239 it was agreed that the elections for the bishop should take place alternately at

Lichfield and Coventry, and at about this time the new polygonal chapter house was started with its fine vestibule, leading from the north choir aisle. Above the chapter house was the treasury and muniment room, which is now the library. This was completed in 1249, and work then began on the complete rebuilding of the nave with, in addition, a magnificent new west front. Lichfield Cathedral was following in style the west fronts of Wells and Salisbury, with their great image screens. Although the feature that particularly links these cathedrals' west fronts is the provision of a hidden passage for singers, whose voices could be heard coming out of concealed holes just above the middle west doorway. By about 1295 the main part of the west front had been finished, and a pair of doors covered in fine decorative ironwork were installed.

Construction then continued, under Bishop Walter de Langton (1296–1321), with the completion of the tops of the three towers and magnificent stone spires. This can be compared with the contemporary work at Salisbury, with its comparable use of ballflower ornament. At about the same time work started on rebuilding the magnificent Lady chapel with very large windows at the east end of the cathedral. These windows were also badly damaged in the English Civil War, and all the original stained glass has been lost. Nevertheless, the chapel is still a structure of great beauty. Hand in hand with this work went the rebuilding of the adjacent retrochoir and presbytery area, which became the setting for an even more grand shrine of St Chad. Once again Lichfield was, on quite a small scale, trying to keep up with the other great shrines of the period. For the final stage of the work in 1337 – linking up the new masonry of the presbytery with the old 13th-century masonry of the choir – the royal master mason, William Ramsey, was called upon; Ramsey was paid 20 shillings (£1) and travelling expenses of 6s. 8d. (33 pence). At this time Ramsey was also working on the new cloister and chapter house at St Paul's, and the Tower of London. Luckily all this work was completed before the Black Death, of which William Ramsey was sadly a victim.

RIGHT: The lower part of the 13th-century west front is one large image screen. The towers and spires that rise above the screen were added in the 14th century, badly damaged in three sieges during the English Civil War and rebuilt in the 1660s.

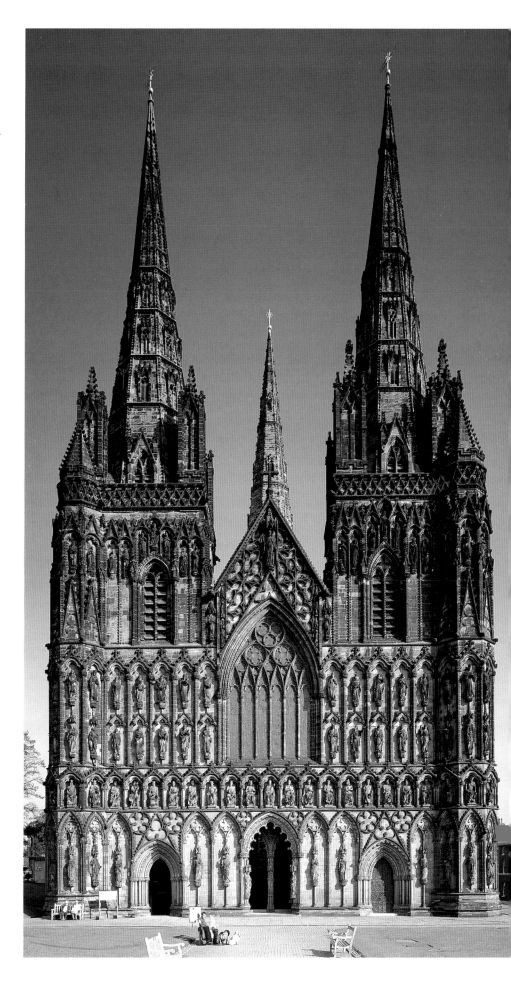

WELLS

SOMERSET

ABOVE: Detail of the *c.* 1320 star vault in the Lady chapel, in the centre of which is the figure of Christ in Glory supported by four angels.

ells Cathedral is perhaps most famous for its magnificent west front, a great image screen that is still covered in just under 300 superb medieval figure sculptures.

Changing fortunes

The first Anglo-Saxon church at Wells was probably built by Bishop Aldhelm in the early 8th century (Aldhelm was the first bishop of the new diocese of Sherborne after it was created in 705), and not long afterwards it was described as 'the minster near the Great Spring at Wells'. In 909 the large diocese of Sherborne was subdivided, and St Andrew's Minster at Wells became a new cathedral. This cathedral probably lay on the site of the present cloister at Wells, with the still-existing

RIGHT: These well-worn, late 13th-century stone steps, which have been trodden for centuries, lead up to the chapter house on the right. In 1459 the higher doorway was made so that the steps could connect directly with the chain bridge that leads to the Vicars' Hall and Close.

ABOVE: The west front with its great image screen containing 297 medieval figures. The towers were added in the late 14th and early 15th centuries, and were made to support spires that were probably never built.

ABOVE: Detail of a buttress on the west front showing a superbly carved medieval statue of a seated bishop in a deep niche. All the slender shafts were originally made of a local stone, Blue Lias, but were replaced in the 19th century with Kilkenny marble.

marketplace to the west of it. To the east are the eponymous springs.

After the Norman Conquest Bishop John de Villula (1088–1122) moved the cathedral to the monastery at Bath, and the Anglo-Saxon cathedral was reduced in status to the church of a college of secular canons. Then, in the mid-12th century, Bishop Robert of Lewes (1136–66) may have rebuilt the church at Wells on the site of the old Anglo-Saxon church. His successor, Bishop Reginald Fitzjocelin (1174–91), an illegitimate son of the bishop of Salisbury, started constructing a completely new building to the north, which he clearly intended to be a new cathedral. This building, the present cathedral, is on a more east–west alignment. Work commenced in about 1176, with the eastern arm and transepts being completed by about 1205. During this time Glastonbury Abbey was forcibly taken over by Bishop Savaric of Bath (1192–1205),

and the see was called the diocese of Bath and Glastonbury. Only in 1219 did it take on the present title of 'Bath and Wells', under the next bishop, Jocelin (1206–42).

Bishop Jocelin determined to complete the building of the new cathedral, and also to build himself a grand new residence immediately to the south of the cathedral. This very fine bishop's palace was later surrounded by defensive curtain walls and a moat, and it is still used by the present bishop of Bath and Wells as his residence. Jocelin's main work in the early years of the reign of King Henry III was to finish the nave and north porch of the cathedral and to build the west front. This happened at exactly the same time as a large new cathedral was being erected in the neighbouring diocese on its new site at Salisbury, and the two buildings clearly influenced one another.

A pioneering style

Wells Cathedral was the earliest in England to evolve a local form of the Gothic style – lancet windows and pointed arches – without any French influence. Even its magnificent west front is very English, and it must be

BELOW: Carved corbel of a lizard or dragon in the north transept near the chapter house steps.

the Anglo-Saxon and Norman church that lay on this site. The old Lady chapel at the east end of this church was, however, retained and rebuilt on the east side of the cloister, though it in turn was also later demolished. A new, octagonal chapter house was also started in the mid-13th century, though unusually it had to be built on the north of the cathedral because of the already existing Lady chapel by the cloister. This chapter house is also unusual because it was built on an undercroft (or crypt) that acted as the treasury or muniment room for the cathedral. There also seems to have been quite a long gap before the magnificent upper chamber, the chapter house itself, was finished at the end of the 13th century. The view up the steep staircase from the north transept to the chapter house doorway is one of the most famous in the whole cathedral.

When the chapter house was completed in about 1306, the cathedral had not finished its building programme, and, just as at Lichfield, a magnificent new scheme was drawn up for a new Lady chapel, retrochoir and small eastern transept chapels. The plan of the Lady chapel is in the form of a flattened octagon, and the wonderful star vault over it, in the shape of a hemi-dome, makes this the most beautiful space in the building.

ABOVE: The amazing strainer arches at the east end of the nave were installed in the 1330s to help support the tower above. The Rood figures on the inverted arch were made in 1920 by G. Tovi to Sir Charles Nicholson's design. Behind the figures is the 15th-century vault under the crossing tower.

remembered that when it was completed in the 1240s, it was not only covered in a mass of carved figure sculpture, but also in painted decoration. Much of this paintwork can be reconstructed from minute samples taken during the recent cleaning and conservation programme.

As the work on the west front was nearing completion, a large new cloister was laid out to the south of the nave. Although this cloister was rebuilt in the 15th century with a library above the east walk, its outer walls are still largely those of the mid-13th century. Oddly enough, the north cloister walk was never built. The laying out of the cloister must have taken place soon after the final demolition of

The work was followed closely by the rebuilding of the whole eastern end, and some fantastic new vaults were put into the whole of the eastern arm as a culmination of the work. While the east end was being rebuilt, money was also found to rebuild the crossing tower, and to add a timber and lead spire to it. The spire was burnt in 1439, however, and the external masonry of the tower was then reworked with a new parapet and pinnacles. Inside the crossing, large scissor strainer arches were put in to help support the weight of the tower. One final addition to the cathedral were the upper western towers, built in the later Middle Ages; these were perhaps originally made for spires.

HEREFORD

HEREFORDSHIRE

n Easter Monday 1786, disaster struck Hereford. The large, early 14th-century west tower collapsed and destroyed the entire west end of the cathedral. The west front was, at that time, the finest late Romanesque façade in England; with its destruction, the only remaining English cathedral with a 12th-century west front was Rochester. After the collapse, a new, very poor west front was made that was set one bay to the east, but to save money no attempt was made to rebuild the tower. In the wake of these rearrangements, the Norman triforium and clerestory of the nave were demolished, and the small spire was removed from the central tower because the walls of the western part of the building were in a dangerous condition after years of neglect. Major restoration work eventually began in Hereford in the mid-19th century, culminating in the rebuilding of the west front by John Oldrid Scott from 1902 to 1908.

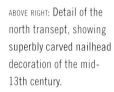

ABOVE RIGHT: Detail of the north transept, showing superbly carved nailhead decoration of the mid-13th century.

LEFT: The view from the south-east shows the vicars' covered walk from their close to the cathedral. The 14th-century tower behind is covered in ballflower and was originally topped with a small timber and lead spire, which James Wyatt removed in the late 18th century.

DEDICATION

- Cathedral Church of the Blessed Virgin Mary and St Ethelbert

HISTORY

- Diocese created for the Magonsaettan c. AD 680
- Norman cathedral built c. 1110–48
- North transept rebuilt in the mid-13th century
- New shrine of St Thomas Cantilupe 1349, destroyed in 1538
- Building of cloister and Vicars' Close in the mid-15th century
- Collapse and rebuilding of the nave 1786–96
- Present west front built 1902–1908

OF SPECIAL INTEREST

- Mappa Mundi and chained library (with 8th-century gospel book)
- Norman font and 12th-century wooden chair
- Thirteenth-century north transept
- Fourteenth-century choir stalls and carved misericords
- Shrine of St Thomas Cantilupe in the north transept
- Chantry chapel of Bishop Audley (c. 1500) on the south side of the Lady chapel
- Bishop's palace to the south, with remains of 12th-century timber arcade in the great hall

Anglo-Saxon origins

The diocese of Hereford was first created in about 680 for a small sub-kingdom of Anglo-Saxons on the Welsh border called the Magonsaettan. In 794 King Ethelbert of East Anglia was murdered near Hereford by King Offa of Mercia, and his tomb soon became the scene of miracles. By the early 9th century there was an important stone church at Hereford, which contained the relics of St Ethelbert. This was enlarged later in the Anglo-Saxon period, but the whole building was destroyed when the Welsh burnt Hereford in 1055. About half a century later construction work began on the present cathedral under Bishop Reinheim (1107–15). Its completion in 1148 was marked by a consecration ceremony under Bishop Robert de Béthune (1131–48).

Despite all the destruction in the late 18th century, the core of the present cathedral is still this early 12th-century building; the fine carved Romanesque work in the presbytery (arcades and triforium), south transept and nave (now only the round pillars and arches) all date from this time, though they were much restored in the 19th century. Probably the most interesting survival is the east wall of the south transept, which also contains the Norman clerestory. Unlike most other Norman transepts it contains no eastern chapels, only a shallow recess in the centre of the wall for an altar. Outside this east wall a treasury (now the sacristy) was built later in the 12th century. At the very end of the 12th century unusual eastern transepts were added to the cathedral. This was probably in connection with the making of a better architectural space for the shrine of St Ethelbert. It was followed in 1220 by the construction of a new eastern Lady chapel, which is again unusual in having a large crypt beneath it. This then led on to the rebuilding of the upper walls of the presbytery and the installation of the fine ribbed vaults.

A Frenchman's vision

In the mid-13th century the bishop of Hereford was a Frenchman, Peter of Aigue-Blanche (1240–68), who had come to England in the retinue of Queen Eleanor of Provence, the wife of King Henry III. As a foreigner he was not much liked, though he was a useful and astute financier for Henry. Peter's great

ABOVE: North side of the nave, with its 12th-century columns and arcade. All the masonry above the arcade was rebuilt in the 19th century.

RIGHT: Shrine of St Thomas Cantilupe in the north transept. Bishop Cantilupe (1275–82) was the last Englishman to be canonized before the Reformation.

contribution to the cathedral was the really magnificent new north transept, which is the finest architectural space in the building. The architecture of the north transept is clearly influenced by Henry III's new French Gothic architecture at Westminster Abbey. Some of the work, such as the immensely tall windows in the west wall, is very striking indeed, as is the bishop's own fine tomb, which can still be seen in the south-east side of the transept. Just to the north of it is another very striking shrine-tomb, which was made in 1287 for the body of Bishop Thomas Cantilupe (1275–82). Less than 40 years after his death the bishop was canonized, and the saint's relics were moved to a new shrine in the Lady chapel in 1349, just after the Black Death hit Hereford.

The popularity of the cult of St Thomas Cantilupe provided extra funds to allow the Romanesque nave and chancel of the cathedral to be given large new windows and ribbed vaults in the late 13th and early 14th centuries. The choir aisles were also given new recesses for the tombs of many of the 12th- and early 13th-century bishops, and, most important of all, two magnificent new towers were built over the crossing and at the west end of the nave. The latter, as we have seen, was destroyed in 1786, but the magnificent crossing tower still survives, and its external decoration has many similarities with the great tower at Salisbury. Once again there is the striking use of many

thousands of ballflowers on the masonry, and the unusual pairs of buttresses on each corner suggest that a stone spire may have been planned but never built.

After the Black Death little new work was done in the cathedral itself, though a fine new vault and south window were put into the south transept in the early 15th century. Much later a beautiful new chantry was made on the south side of the Lady chapel by Bishop Audley (c. 1500), and an elaborate outer chamber was added to the north porch by bishops Mayhew and Booth in 1516–19. Both buildings are outstanding examples of the latest Gothic architecture of the early Tudor period.

ABOVE: The 13th-century Lady chapel was restored in the mid-19th century. The east window, which is a memorial to Dean Mereweather (1832–50), has exceptionally fine Victorian glass.

ABOVE LEFT: The triforium of the north transept, showing the tracery that is derived directly from the Westminster Abbey triforium (although the arches here are even more triangular).

HENRY VIII'S NEW CATHEDRALS

The first ideas on creating new cathedrals in England were perhaps formulated by Cardinal Wolsey in the 1520s, but after his fall in 1529 nothing more happened for over a decade. Then, in 1540, the king himself wrote that, it was 'most expedient, and necessary that more bishoprics, collegiate and cathedral churches' should be made from the resources of the dissolved houses, and a document still survives, in the king's own hand, of 'Bishoprics to be made'. This is a list of 13 possible new dioceses and the places that could become cathedrals. From this list only four places were chosen: Peterborough, Westminster Abbey, St Peter's Abbey, Gloucester and Oseney Abbey at Oxford. As we shall see, the cathedral at Oxford was soon moved to Christ Church, and Chester Abbey and the oddity of the Augustinian abbey at Bristol were later added to the list. No further cathedrals were made, no doubt because Henry VIII needed the money for himself. Like the medieval monastic cathedrals, new deans and chapters were created with major and minor canons and attached schools. All of these new cathedrals survive today except Westminster, which ceased to be a cathedral in 1556.

ABOVE: King Henry VIII confirming Bishop Sherburne as bishop of Chichester in 1508, as painted by Lambert Barnard in Chichester Cathedral *c.* 1520. RIGHT: The enormous mid-14th-century east window dominates Gloucester Cathedral. On the left, the vertical Perpendicular panelling is set against the round arches of the Norman arcade and triforium.

GEORGE FREDERICK HANDEL Efq:
born February. XXIII MDCLXXXIV.
MDCCLIX. LFRoubiliac inv.et sc.

WESTMINSTER ABBEY

LONDON

DEDICATION

- Collegiate Church of St Peter

HISTORY

- A Benedictine abbey from AD 959
- Rebuilt by King Edward the Confessor c. 1050–66
- Coronation church since 1066
- Rebuilt by King Henry III 1245–70, with a new shrine to St Edward (canonized in 1161)
- Burial place of many kings and queens 1066–1760
- Cathedral from 1540 to 1556, and since 1559 a Royal Peculiar
- Burial place of many famous people from the 17th to 19th centuries
- Western towers completed under Nicholas Hawksmoor 1740–45
- Cleaning and restoration of western towers and Henry VII chapel 1973–95

OF SPECIAL INTEREST

- The great pavement, shrine and tomb of Henry III all with Italian Cosmati work (1268–9)
- Tombs and monuments to medieval kings around the shrine of St Edward
- Henry VII chapel with original stalls and Tudor royal tombs
- Henry V's chantry chapel with, beneath it, the coronation chair
- Poets' Corner monuments (south transept) and statesmen's monuments (north transept)

ABOVE: This fine statue by Roubiliac of Handel with music from *The Messiah* sits on the west wall of Poets' Corner in the south transept.

estminster Abbey is probably the most famous church in England, but what is little known is that it became a cathedral in 1540 in its own diocese of Middlesex. This diocese had a life of only 10 years, but Westminster remained as a 'cathedral church and episcopal see to the bishop of London', as a contemporary document puts it, for some six more years (1550–56), before being made an abbey once again by Queen Mary. With the accession of Queen Elizabeth, the abbey was finally suppressed and in July 1559 it became a new collegiate church, with a dean and canons who were answerable only to the monarch. This 'Royal Peculiar', as it is called, survives to this day.

An abbey fit for kings

For well over 900 years, Westminster Abbey has been the place of coronation for the sovereign, but the first church here was perhaps the new

RIGHT: The newly cleaned western towers were finished by Nicholas Hawksmoor in the 1740s, yet they sit upon uncompleted 16th-century work. The bottom 50 feet of the towers date from the early 12th century, though evidence of this ancient building now lies behind the huge Portland stone plinth.

ABOVE: The incomparable Lady chapel has splendid fan vaulting and suspended pendant vaults – architecture at its very best. The magnificent raised stalls are now used by the Knights of the Bath.

Benedictine abbey founded by St Dunstan (then bishop of London) in about 959. Tradition takes the foundation back to the early 7th century, but this is unlikely. The monastery west of the City of London – hence its name, Westminster – first became really important when King Edward the Confessor built a large new Norman church here in the 1050s. His death and funeral in the new abbey, early in 1066, is shown on the Bayeux Tapestry, while William the Conqueror's coronation also took place here on Christmas Day 1066. Since then all English monarchs have been crowned here, and until the mid-18th century many of them were also buried here, in the area around the shrine of St Edward the Confessor (the king was canonized in 1163).

ABOVE: The Purbeck marble shrine of St Edward the Confessor is decorated in Cosmati work and covered by a 16th-century canopy. Beyond Edward's shrine is the tomb of Henry V, beneath the statuary of Henry's own chantry chapel.

ABOVE RIGHT: The south-east chapel in the Henry VII chapel has fine frieze fenestration. The tomb and effigy by Westmacott on the left is of Antoine Philippe, duc de Montpellier and brother of the future King Louis XVIII of France. The duke died in exile in England in 1807.

RIGHT: This fine bronzework is to be found on the wonderful screen that surrounds the tomb of Henry VII.

Little now survives of the great Norman church – though walls of some of the Norman monastic buildings around the cloister can still be seen – because an immense new church was started by Henry III in July 1245. This wonderful building was very much in the French Gothic style, with new traceried windows and a vault that was over 100 feet above the floor. This vault was the highest in England, though many French cathedrals had vaults that went even higher. For about 10 years huge sums of money were spent on the work, and most of the eastern arm, including the great aisled transepts, was built. The large new octagonal chapter house and the north-east part of the cloister, which were joined to the abbey, were also built at this time. Work continued on the eastern part of the nave, to house the monks' stalls, although this was at a much slower rate, due to lack of funds. After many delays, caused largely by political problems, a great service was held in the abbey on 13 October 1269, when the relics of St Edward were translated to a sumptuous new shrine behind the high altar, and mass was celebrated at that altar for the first time. Work proceeded for a few more years, and when Henry III died in 1272 it is thought some £50,000 had been spent on the new abbey (many hundreds of millions of pounds at today's prices), making it by far the most expensive building project in Europe at this time.

A new nave

When Edward I came to the throne, work on completing the project ceased, though Henry III was buried in a magnificent tomb to the north of the shrine. This was followed by the tombs of most of the later medieval English kings and queens for the next century and a half.

In 1375 a new fund was set up at the instigation of Cardinal Langham, a former abbot of Westminster and archbishop of Canterbury, who was then at the papal court in Avignon; the following year work began on demolishing the old nave, though this was done very slowly. Then, for 16 years from 1387, the massive new Purbeck marble piers were built at the west end of the nave, followed by the arcades and aisle vaults, with financial help from Richard II. This was at exactly the same time as the nave of Canterbury Cathedral was being rebuilt, though the work at Canterbury was finished long before that at Westminster, thanks to support from the next king, Henry IV, who was eventually buried at Canterbury. Work on the triforium levels continued under Henry V (1413–22), but then lapsed until the work on the nave, with its high vaults (104 feet above the ground), was finally completed between 1468 and 1505. Without royal patronage the monks could only find a small amount of money each year. Abbot John Islip (1500–32) was determined to finish the work on the western towers, but after his death and the dissolution of the monastery in 1540, they were left unfinished. The towers were not completed until the 1740s, when Nicholas Hawksmoor was employed to work on them.

Just when the nave was being finished off, a truly remarkable addition was made at the east end, once again entirely paid for by a king, Henry VII. This was the new Lady chapel (or Henry VII's chapel, as it is now generally called), perhaps the most remarkable architecture in the whole of Westminster Abbey. It was put up between 1503 and 1509, the year in which the king died, and Henry VII gave about £20,000 for its building costs – once again a huge sum for the time. The chapel was built to contain not only the burials of Henry VII and his queen, but also a new shrine for the murdered King Henry VI. In the event, Henry VI's body remained at St George's Chapel, Windsor. The final stage of the building work in the new Lady chapel was the vaults, and these are certainly the most magnificent examples ever built in England.

RIGHT: The view south across the transept to Poets' Corner. The great rose window was completed in the mid-15th century.

PETERBOROUGH
CAMBRIDGESHIRE

ABOVE: Detail of royal master mason John Wastell's fan vault in the 'New Building' (1496–1508).

BELOW: The three vast arches of the magnificent 13th-century west front dwarf the central late 14th-century Trinity chapel and Galilee porch.

he diocese of Peterborough was created at the same time as the dioceses of Gloucester and Oxford, on 3 September 1541. It was cut from the middle of the huge diocese of Lincoln, and covered the counties of Northampton and Rutland. The large cathedral, 481 feet long, was a great Benedictine abbey church built largely in the 12th century. A smooth transition was made possible after the dissolution of the abbey in 1539, because the last abbot, John Chambers (who was appointed by Cardinal Wolsey), became the first bishop and four of the senior monks became canons. The new bishop was therefore able to stay in his fine house to the south-west of the cathedral, which is still the bishop's palace. The cathedral had been the burial place several years earlier, in 1536, of Henry VIII's first wife, Catherine of Aragon. Ironically, Mary Queen of Scots was also buried here in 1587, following her execution at nearby Fotheringhay Castle. The queens lay on either side of the presbytery near the high altar until Mary's son, James I, came to the throne and united the two kingdoms; James ordered that his mother's body be removed to Westminster Abbey, and this was carried out in 1612.

Seventh-century origins

The first abbey was founded on this important site, on the edge of the Fens and originally called Medeshamstede, by King Peada of Mercia in the mid-7th century. Two centuries afterwards it was destroyed by the Vikings, before being refounded as a new abbey by Æthelwold, bishop of Winchester, in about 965. Traces of the east end of this abbey church were found in the late 19th century under the south transept: the nave of the church lay beneath the later north cloister walk.

In the later Anglo-Saxon period the abbey and its associated town were fortified, and its name was changed from Medeshamstede to Peterborough, after the name of the abbey's patron saint. The Anglo-Saxon abbey church was finally destroyed in a great fire in 1116, and rebuilding started two years later under Abbot John de Séez. Along with Ely,

Bury St Edmunds and Norwich, this was one of four vast Benedictine abbey churches in the area around the Fens, all of them being built in the monumental Romanesque style. At Peterborough work started as usual on the eastern arm, and the presbytery and transepts (each with three eastern chapels) were probably complete by 1143 when Alexander, bishop of Lincoln, consecrated the church. Much of the eastern apse of the Norman church still survives, though flanked by the 'New Building', because a new 13th-century eastern arm was never built here. Instead, a very large Lady chapel was put up on the east side of the north transept in 1272–90. Sadly it was demolished in the mid-17th century.

Work on completing the very long 11-bay nave took much longer, and it is likely that this was not finished until about 1180, when two western towers were being started. Then, in the early 13th century, an extraordinary new west front was added to the building, which had three giant arches with vaults behind them. Above the arches were three highly decorated gables – with tall turrets for staircases on either side – which received stone spires later in the 13th century. Peterborough's wonderful west front is in part developed from the west front of Lincoln Minster, but because it is an addition to the Romanesque nave, it is entirely Gothic with no earlier work showing through. While the west front was being completed, a magnificent new painted wooden ceiling was put into the nave. This very long boarded structure is now being cleaned and conserved.

Finishing touches

The whole building was finally completed by 1238, when the great bishop of Lincoln, Robert Grosseteste, consecrated it. After this only minor building works were carried out, with the exception of the great Lady chapel. A beautiful little Galilee porch, with a chapel above, was inserted into the centre of the west front in the late 14th century, while various windows, particularly those in the west front, were enlarged and given tracery. One final addition, still called the 'New Building' 500 years after it was built, is the beautiful ambulatory around the east end. It has large windows and is covered by fan vaults, just like those put into King's College Chapel, Cambridge. This work was paid for by Abbot Robert Kirkton (1496–1508).

During the English Civil War, 1643–50, much damage was inflicted on the cathedral by parliamentary soldiers. They also took down the cloister and Lady chapel to use the materials (stone and lead) elsewhere. In the later 19th century, by contrast, much beauty was restored to the cathedral, and J. L. Pearson's fine marble floor, in a 'Cosmati' style, and great ciborium over the high altar, also inspired by Italian work, are particularly fine.

ABOVE: Burial place of Queen Catherine of Aragon, first wife of Henry VIII, in the north choir aisle. After her divorce Catherine left court, and died at nearby Kimbolton in 1536. The fine ironwork over the tomb, by White & Son of London, was installed in 1894 after J. L. Pearson's great restoration. In the foreground is one of the large early 12th-century pillars, while the fan vaulting of the 'New Building' can be seen in the distance on the left.

OXFORD
OXFORDSHIRE

DEDICATION

- Cathedral Church of Christ

HISTORY

- Late Anglo-Saxon church built here
- Henry I established Augustinian priory in 1122
- Present church built *c.* 1160–1200, with 13th- and 14th-century additions, and new shrine in 1289
- Priory suppressed by Wolsey, who started to build Cardinal College 1525–9
- Henry VIII's College 1532–46
- Cathedral moved from Oseney to St Frideswide's (Christ Church) in 1546
- Charles I based at Christ Church during English Civil War 1642–6
- The Revd Charles Lutwidge Dodgson (Lewis Carroll) was a mathematics tutor at Christ Church and Alice Liddell's father was dean in the mid-19th century
- Major restoration 1870–76 by Sir George Gilbert Scott

OF SPECIAL INTEREST

- Reconstructed late 13th-century shrine of St Frideswide (1890), and watching loft (*c.* 1500) to south
- Early 12th-century chapter house
- Fourteenth-century monuments in Lady chapel
- Sixteenth- and 17th-century monuments, including that of Robert King, last abbot of Oseney and first bishop
- Many new furnishings of the 1870s

ABOVE: Detail of the fine pendant vault in the choir, with Sir George Gilbert Scott's Norman-style rose east window of *c.* 1875.

he cathedral at Christ Church, Oxford, is the smallest in England, though it is still a cruciform structure with some fine architecture. It also has a very strange and complicated history, and is still the only cathedral that doubles as a college chapel.

In the later Anglo-Saxon period there was a nunnery here, in the south-east corner of the fortified town of Oxford, which had been founded by St Frideswide in the 8th century. This was burnt down by the Danes in 1002, and then refounded as an Augustinian priory, as was Carlisle Cathedral, in 1122. Parts of the chapter house here date from not long after this, but the present church was probably not started until about 1160. It was designed to have double aisles in the nave and chancel and in the transepts, and on its north-east side a special chapel was created, and was ready by 1180 for the shrine of St Frideswide. The architecture, with its large round pillars and finely carved capitals, is of the latest Romanesque, and when the building was finished it probably had a seven-bay nave.

In 1524 Cardinal Wolsey decided, however, that the area around St Frideswide's Priory would be the ideal site for his vast new college. He dissolved the priory and 21 other small religious houses so that he could use all their lands to build and endow this new college, Cardinal College. Work got under way in July 1525, and a huge base court was laid out, which required the western half of the nave of St Frideswide's to be demolished. Then, with 500 men, he built a great new hall and kitchen to the south of the court. He also started to lay out a very large chapel on the north side to replace St Frideswide's and to rival King's College Chapel, Cambridge. In 1529, though, as is well known, Wolsey fell from favour and all work stopped. The college of 20 scholars had already been set up, and Henry VIII decided in

ABOVE: The east end of the cathedral and Lady chapel. In the background is the early 13th-century tower and spire, which sit above the crossing.

LEFT: The nave looking west; its inward facing pews and alternating round and octagonal piers resemble the choir at Canterbury.

1532 to refound it as Henry VIII's College, but did not pay for any more building work – hence the unfinished state of the college today.

Meanwhile, another large Augustinian house to the west of Oxford, Oseney Abbey, was dissolved in 1539. Just over three years later the great church became a cathedral, with the abbot, Robert King, becoming the first bishop of Oxford. Virtually no trace of Oseney Abbey, which was situated just south of where Oxford railway station now stands, is visible, as in November 1546, not long before his death, Henry VIII decided to refound his college yet

again as Christ Church College, with a dean and eight canons, and at the same time to transfer the bishop's *cathedra* from Oseney to St Frideswide's. This allowed the king to acquire for himself the whole of Oseney Abbey and all its estates. The last reminder of the abbey is its large bell, 'Great Tom', which was brought to Christ Church and hangs in the tower built by Sir Christopher Wren in 1681 over the unfinished gateway to Christ Church. This, and the fine early 13th-century tower with its stone spire over the cathedral, are now two of the famous 'dreaming spires' of Oxford.

GLOUCESTER
GLOUCESTERSHIRE

DEDICATION

- Cathedral Church of St Peter and the Holy and Indivisible Trinity

HISTORY

- Abbey church built by Serlo 1089–1100
- Murder of Edward II at Berkeley Castle and burial here in 1327
- Rebuilding of eastern arm, including great east window (72 by 38 feet), 1331–50
- Rebuilding of cloister, transepts, west front, south porch, crossing tower and Lady chapel 1388–1499
- New bishop, dean and canons created in 1541

OF SPECIAL INTEREST

- Early Norman crypt
- Tombs and effigies of Robert Curthose and Edward II
- Fourteenth-century presbytery with high vault and great east window
- Organ case of 1665 (still in situ on choir screen)
- Choir stalls below crossing
- Large 15th-century Lady chapel, with western bridge and whispering gallery
- Fan-vaulted cloister with monks' carrels and lavatorium
- Norman and 14th-century chapter house and other monastic buildings

ABOVE: The pillars in the centre of the early Norman crypt date from *c*. 1089. The ground level of the crypt was later raised, and massive extra ribs and vaults were inserted in the early 14th century to take the weight of the new choir.

he great abbey church of St Peter at Gloucester is, as are Durham or Winchester, one of the most magnificent Benedictine churches in England. It became a cathedral in 1541 because it contained 'famous monuments of our renowned ancestors, kings of England', as the Act of Parliament puts it. Most famous is the superb tomb of Edward II, the victim of a murder in nearby Berkeley Castle in 1327. The abbey church also had the fine effigy of Robert Curthose, Duke of Normandy and eldest son of William the Conqueror, and the monument of King Osric, the founder of the abbey in about 681. King Osric's monument had been ordered by Abbot Parker only a few years before the Dissolution.

Background to the modern cathedral

Not long after the Conquest in 1072, a Norman abbot called Serlo was appointed and started to rebuild the present great church in 1089. By the beginning of the 12th century there were 60 monks, and the eastern part of the building must have been complete. Work on the eight- or nine-bay nave, with its magnificent great round pillars, was finished by 1120, and the consecration of the whole building took place the following year. Work then continued on the neighbouring monastic buildings. In 1216 the nine-year-old Henry III was crowned in the abbey, and over the next 30 years the central tower was rebuilt and fine stone vaulting was inserted into the nave. Then, in the early 14th century, the nave south aisle was rebuilt and the Norman eastern arm was given many fine new traceried windows.

RIGHT: The 13th-century effigy of Robert Curthose, Duke of Normandy and eldest son of William the Conqueror, lies in the south ambulatory. Robert was held prisoner by his brother King Henry I for 28 years. When he finally died, at Cardiff Castle in 1134, he was an old man of 80, and was allowed to be buried in state in front of the abbey's high altar.

BELOW: The beautiful fan vaulting and stained-glass windows of the east walk of the great cloister make this one of the most breathtaking areas of the cathedral. In the south walk the monks had their carrels (working desks), while in the north walk was the lavatorium, where they washed before going into the refectory.

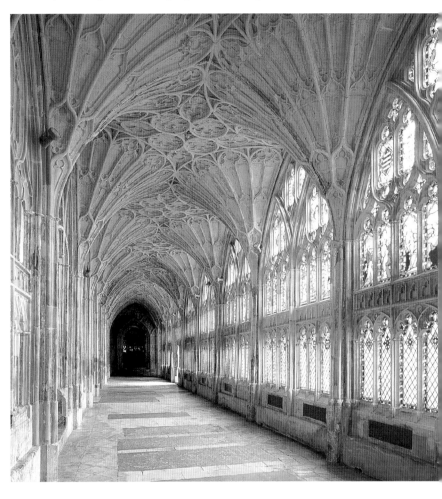

ABOVE: The cathedral from the north-west corner of the cloister, with the chapter house on the left. The beautiful 225-foot-high crossing tower of the late 15th century dominates the cathedral.

With the murder of Edward II, and his burial in the abbey (the nearby abbey of Bristol refused to take the corpse), the church became a place of pilgrimage and was also granted many privileges by Edward III. As a result, the south transept and then the presbytery were remodelled from the 1330s in a spectacular way, using the new Perpendicular style of architecture. The inner walls of the amazing presbytery, on its Norman crypt, were impressively refaced and then covered with a very fine new lierne vault. Even more remarkably the east wall behind the high altar was knocked out and replaced with the largest window possible (even larger than the great east window of York Minster), creating simply a wall of glass. It is cleverly contrived in three separate vertical planes like a triptych, built across the Norman apse, and behind it runs a masonry tunnel to link the triforia to the Lady chapel gallery. The glazing of this huge window – perhaps in part a memorial for the Battle of Crécy – was probably just finished by the time of the Black Death, 1348–50 (see page 81).

Soon after the Black Death the cloisters were rebuilt, and here we see the earliest fan vaulting in England in what is perhaps the most beautiful cloister in the country. Work continued on the north transept and at the west end of the nave, and then in the 1450s the wonderful new crossing tower was built; this, too, is one of the finest in Britain. The final great achievement of the late 15th century is the magnificent eastern Lady chapel, which is once again a superb architectural space in which polyphonic Lady masses were sung for nearly 50 years. This ingenious building simply had to become a cathedral.

BRISTOL

BRISTOL

ABOVE: George Edmund
Street's western
towers, built 1884–8,
were designed in 1876
amid controversy
surrounding the
addition of 'papist'
statues – such as
St Gregory crowned
with a papal tiara –
on the outside of
the cathedral.

ristol Cathedral is something of an anomaly. It probably became a cathedral because the powerful governing class in the city in the mid-16th century suggested it to the king. It did not feature in Henry VIII's original list of new dioceses, and when it was created in 1542, the diocese consisted of the city and small county of Bristol and the quite separate and detached county of Dorset, which was taken from the Salisbury diocese. From 1836 to 1897 it was joined to Gloucester diocese, with the bishop having two cathedrals.

A Victorian reworking

The cathedral today owes much to the 19th century. The nave was completely rebuilt after 1868 by George Edmund Street, and this was followed by a complete Victorian reordering of the interior by J. L. Pearson and his son in 1890–1900. Despite this, the early 14th-century eastern arm of the building remains one of the most interesting and splendid structures in the country.

RIGHT: The remarkable
south choir aisle vault
was built soon after
1298. Its east window,
however, is a more
recent addition (1962)
by stained-glass artist
Keith New, and shows
the Holy Spirit. New
also designed some
of the windows
in the nave of
Coventry Cathedral.

The abbey, for Augustinian canons, was founded here in about 1140 on the west side of the River Frome (then the port) from the great city of Bristol. Part of the south transept and most of the magnificent rib-vaulted chapter house and its vestibule date from soon after this, and show that a large abbey church, with its cloister on the south, was being built here from about 1150 to 1170. Early in the 13th century a fine Lady chapel, now called the Elder Lady chapel, with a stone vault was added to the east side of the north transept. This chapel's architecture has affinities with the western part of Wells Cathedral.

The great rebuilding of the eastern arm was carried out under Abbot Knowle (1306–32), who had earlier, from 1298, been the treasurer of the abbey. Everything about the eastern arm is unusual. First, it is a hall-church – that is, a building with all three aisles of similar height and under one roof. What is more, the vaults are completely different from any others: in the aisles is a series of open cross-arches which support extraordinary double-vaults set sideways. On the south-east side of the south aisle, in the vestibule to the Berkeley chapel, is an even more extraordinary vault with flying ribs and large decorated bosses, with a flat ribbed-ceiling visible above it. The main central vault is equally unusual, and has tiercerons and very early lierne ribs, and no ridge rib. The windows contain fine Decorated tracery: the great east window (also the east window of the Lady chapel) is an extraordinary mixture of Decorated tracery with, at the top, a 'nastily spreading trefoil', in the memorable words of architectural historian Sir Nikolaus Pevsner.

All of this precocious work was finished by the 1330s, and then after a pause of nearly a century and a half, work started on refacing the 12th-century transepts and crossing in the Perpendicular style. A large new tower was also built above the crossing, and in the early 16th century the nave was demolished, and work on its rebuilding was put in hand. Unfortunately, this was never completed, so that when the church became a cathedral in 1542 the nave was still a building site. This meant that the whole of the new cathedral had to be fitted into the eastern arm, so the high altar was moved to the east wall of the Lady chapel and a new choir screen (reused from the Whitefriars church in Bristol) was inserted two bays east of the crossing. This lasted for 350 years until Pearson's reordering of the whole cathedral in the late 19th century.

ABOVE RIGHT: Street's nave of 1868–77 with Pearson's choir screen (1905). The choir and sanctuary beyond were restored in 1899, and above them is an amazing early 14th-century lierne vault.

RIGHT: The Lady chapel was repainted in 1935, revivifying on the east wall the shields of Clare (left) and England (three lions), the head possibly of Edward II, and, in the later frieze above, the initials and rebus of William Burton (1526–39), the last abbot.

CHESTER
CHESHIRE

ABOVE: Detail of a wooden carved figure in the late 14th-century choir stalls.

BELOW: The cathedral as seen from the south-west. All the pinnacles, flying buttresses and turrets date from Scott's 19th-century restoration.

rom the late Anglo-Saxon period, there were two important churches at Chester – the church of St Werburgh inside the north-east corner of the Roman fortress walls, and the church of St John the Baptist next to the Roman amphitheatre, just outside the south-east corner of the Roman walls. In 1075 the bishop of Lichfield moved his seat to St John's Church, probably still an Anglo-Saxon building, and for about the next 20 years this was the cathedral for the diocese. With the move to the wealthy abbey at Coventry in 1095, St John's Church ceased to be the cathedral, though the bishop kept a presence here, and the diocese was often called 'Coventry, Lichfield and Chester' in the later Middle Ages. At just about the time of the removal of the bishop's seat from Chester, the Church of St Werburgh was rebuilt and turned into the new Benedictine abbey of St Werburgh. It was this church that Henry VIII made into a cathedral in 1541, after the dissolution of the abbey. The new diocese was cut out of the western part of York diocese and the northern part of Coventry and Lichfield (see map on page 157).

A 450-year project

The Chester Cathedral of today is a fine medieval and early Tudor building which was built, and then rebuilt, in many stages from about 1090 until the Dissolution in 1540. It was, also, however, rather over-restored in the 19th century. The oldest surviving parts of the Norman abbey church can be seen along the north side of the church, and include the north transept and the base of the north-west tower. North of this, the cloister and several of the monastic buildings still exist, including the early 13th-century chapter house and its striking vestibule with shafts that run straight up to become vault ribs. The cloisters were rebuilt only a few years before the dissolution, and the positions of the monks' carrels (writing desks) in the south and west walks can still be seen. The eastern arm of the church was completely rebuilt in the 13th century, with the new shrine of St Werburgh at its centre, and a new Lady chapel to the east.

In the years before 1300 Chester was the centre for Edward I's conquest of Wales and his subsequent castle-

building programme there, and this was when the choir was rebuilt. It still contains very fine late 14th-century canopied monks' stalls with wonderful misericords. At this time the nave was also being rebuilt, as well as the highly unusual large double-aisled south transept, which formerly held the church of St Oswald. It is also worth noting that most of the vaults, apart from that of the Lady chapel, are of wood, as in York Minster, rather than stone.

In the last half century before the Dissolution of the Monasteries, a great deal of building work took place, including the cloisters, already mentioned, and the fine lantern tower. A large new south-west tower with its neighbouring porch – the main entry to the cathedral from the town – was started but never finished. It now contains the bishop's consistory court, and its 17th-century fittings are a unique survival in England.

ABOVE: The panel depicting the miracle at the wedding at Cana, from the Wardell window of 1890 in St Oswald's chapel.

RIGHT: The fine masonry above the high altar was built in several stages at the end of the 13th century, while the shrine of St Werburgh stood just behind the high altar until 1538.

WREN'S BAROQUE
MASTERPIECE

The great cathedral church of St Paul in the City of London is probably
now the most famous cathedral in Britain. Its fame rests on the fact
that it was designed by Sir Christopher Wren, and completed during
his lifetime – Wren died in 1723, aged 91, as his very modest memorial
in the crypt tells us. The cathedral took 35 years to build, from 1675 to
1710, and is unique in being the only completely new cathedral to be
built between Salisbury in the early 13th century and Liverpool in the
20th century. Truro Cathedral – see pages 121–2 – incorporated a small
part of the earlier church in its fabric. It is also the only cathedral built
in the English Baroque style, with a huge, instantly recognizable dome,
which at 365 feet high (including the cross on the top) once dominated
the City of London. Sadly the course of the 20th century detracted from
the impression made by the dome as numerous taller buildings were
erected in the cathedral's environs.

ABOVE: Nelson's tomb, which lies in the crypt, uses the 16th-century sarcophagus that was made for Cardinal Wolsey.
RIGHT: From the south-east, the cathedral can still be seen in isolated glory, seemingly untouched by the modern
developments that lie all around it.

ST PAUL'S

LONDON

DEDICATION

- Cathedral Church of St Paul

HISTORY

- First church built here in AD 604
- Rebuilt by first Norman bishop, Maurice, from 1087
- Large Romanesque cathedral finished by *c.* 1150
- Very large new eastern arm, with shrine for St Erkenwald, built *c.* 1250–1314
- Inigo Jones recased cathedral and added west portico 1633–40
- Great Fire of London and destruction of old St Paul's in 1666
- Wren's new cathedral built 1675–1710

OF SPECIAL INTEREST

- Effigy of John Donne, in his shroud, from the old cathedral
- The Great Model
- The 'whispering gallery', dome and lantern
- Choir stalls by Grinling Gibbons
- Nelson's tomb in crypt (and monument above)
- Duke of Wellington's tomb in crypt (and huge nave monument above)
- Sir Christopher Wren's tomb (and small plaque) in crypt

ABOVE: Detail of the painted stucco work and late Victorian mosaic on the chancel.

RIGHT: The modern altar on the east side of the crossing. Behind it stand Grinling Gibbons's choir stalls and the organ, which was commissioned in 1694 from Bernard Schmidt, alias Father Smith, and stood until 1860 on a solid choir screen. After the screen was removed the case was divided into two halves in 1872.

he history of St Paul's goes back much further in time than Wren's great building – back to the year 604, when the first cathedral was constructed under a monk called Mellitus who came to England with St Augustine of Canterbury and became the first bishop of the East and Middle Saxons. London should have been the metropolitical see, but because of the political situation at the beginning of the 7th century Canterbury became, and has remained ever since, the seat of the archbishop. Nothing is yet known about the Anglo-Saxon cathedral, which was finally destroyed in 1087. A completely new cathedral was then started by Bishop Maurice, and only the eastern arm of this cathedral was completed by the beginning of the 12th century. The next bishop, Richard (1108–27), put most of his own income towards the building of a very fine long nave of 12 bays (he was clearly influenced by Winchester Cathedral). Completed by the mid-12th century, the nave survived intact until the Great Fire in 1666, though it was refaced externally by Inigo Jones in the early 17th century (Jones also refaced the west front and added a huge west portico).

The cathedral grows apace

In the middle of the 13th century work started on building a vast new eastern arm on a greatly enlarged crypt, and this was clearly to house a splendid new shrine for the relics of St Erkenwald (a late 7th-century bishop). The work on the new fabric was complete by 1314, but another decade or so was needed before the canons' choir and the new shrine were finished. In 1315 a very large timber-framed spire (covered in lead) was erected on top of the already tall 13th-century crossing tower, so that by the mid-14th century St Paul's had become the longest and tallest cathedral in Europe. The total length of 585 feet now exceeded Winchester, and the height of the top of the spire was said to be 489 feet, making it just taller than the Great Pyramid in Egypt. One final addition of the 1330s was the remarkable two-storeyed cloister in the angle between the south transept and the nave. In the centre of this was an extraordinary two-storeyed octagonal chapter house. (Fragments of the south side of the foundation of this cloister can still be glimpsed in the flower-beds in the south side of Wren's nave.) The spire was destroyed by lightning in 1561, but most of the rest of this incomparable medieval building survived until the Great Fire of 1666 when it was, of course, gutted. The massive shell was then demolished in stages over the next decade.

The arrival of Wren

During the English Civil War, 1643–50, the cathedral was badly treated, and soon after the Restoration a royal commission was appointed to look into the state of the fabric. It was soon discovered that the central tower

ABOVE: The inner dome, made of plaster-faced brick, was decorated with Thornhill's monochrome early 18th-century paintings.

ABOVE RIGHT: The view, at gallery level, right down the nave and chancel from the west end. In the distance is the 1958 baldacchino of Dykes Bower and Allen.

RIGHT: This detail is taken from one of Tijou's superb ironwork gate-screens, which were made in the 1690s. They now flank the sanctuary and are set in frames made by Bodley & Garner in 1890.

and its supporting piers were the biggest problem, and it was suggested that they should be demolished and rebuilt. By this time the young Christopher Wren had joined the Commission, and in May 1666 he came up with the ingenious idea of removing the crossing piers altogether, or as Wren himself wrote: 'cutting off the inner corners of the cross, to reduce this middle part into a spacious dome or rotundo with a cupola or hemispherical roof'. Here is

the first mention of the unique dome, and the idea of removing the crossing piers perhaps came to him at Ely, where his uncle was bishop. (After the collapse of the crossing tower at Ely in 1322, the monks had replaced it with an irregular octagon surrounded by a lantern.) Wren's idea was accepted, but only a few days later the whole cathedral was engulfed and gutted by the Great Fire.

After the fire nearly a decade was spent deciding what to do. Wren produced several designs, all of which were too radical for the authorities – a whole series of drawings and models, including the magnificent 'Great Model', survive to show how the design evolved. Eventually he produced a much more conservative scheme, with a new long nave, transepts and chancel, but still with a dome (on top of which was a strange-looking spire). Wren clearly did not like this scheme, and when it received the Royal Warrant in May 1675 he was given a 'let-out' clause 'to make some variations, rather ornamental, than essential, as from time to time he should see proper'. As a result he was able to redesign his new cathedral piecemeal as it was being erected over the next 30 years.

New foundations

The foundation stone, in the south-east corner of the building, was laid on 21 June 1675, and work progressed fairly rapidly, with the transept ends being started in 1681 and the outer walls of the nave laid out in 1684. The foundations for the west front were dug two years later, and by this time Wren had considerably remodelled the plan in the Royal Warrant. The new cathedral was 510 feet long and on a different, slightly more north-eastern alignment than its predecessor. The eastern arm was reaching completion in 1694, and was finally consecrated in 1697, after much complaint about how long it was taking. The upper parts of the transepts were completed the following year, and a few months later the Morning chapel (now St Dunstan's chapel) on the north-west side of the nave came into use. The final designs for the west towers and the dome were still evolving at this time, and it was not until 1704 that the final design for the completion of the dome, or 'great cupola', seems to have been drawn up. On top of the great drum over the crossing, a brick cone was built, onto which was fixed the timber frame for the dome. This was then covered in the traditional material, lead. A great lantern was put on top of this, surmounted by a gilded orb and cross. The western towers were built from 1705 to 1708, and with the completion of the dome in 1710 the whole building was at last finished. It had cost £738,845 5s. 2d. – such specific accounts were demanded by parliament – and was largely paid for by a tax on coal coming into the Port of London.

BELOW: The newly cleaned and conserved Great Model was made in 1673–4 by William Cleere, the master joiner, and is one of the most splendid architectural models ever made.

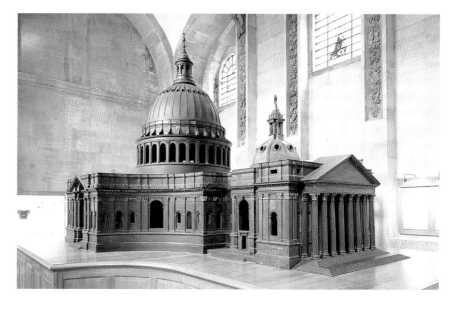

THE NINETEENTH CENTURY

The Industrial Revolution left the Church of England far behind, and by the time that the first tentative steps were being taken to create new dioceses at Ripon (1836) and Manchester (1847), England had some huge new cities like Birmingham and Liverpool, which had few churches and no cathedrals. Even in the later 19th century, when first Truro and St Alban's dioceses, and then Liverpool, Newcastle, Southwell and Wakefield were created, there was no real drive to build totally new cathedrals, except in remote Cornwall. By contrast, the Roman Catholic church, with very little money, started to build churches in the new urban centres after their 'emancipation' in 1829, and with the restoration of the Catholic hierarchy in 1850, new dioceses and cathedrals were quickly created. Much more effort went into the restoration of the great medieval cathedrals in the later 19th century, after their deans and chapters had been woken up, and slowly reformed. The most important change was the setting up of the Ecclesiastical Commission in the 1830s; this started the redistribution of the Church's great assets (particularly its great landed wealth) to allow a reformed diocesan system to be created.

ABOVE: The Lamb of God as depicted in an iron screen at Southwark Roman Catholic Cathedral.
RIGHT: The Blessed Sacrament chapel at Nottingham Roman Catholic Cathedral was superbly decorated to A. W. N. Pugin's designs in 1884 and carefully restored in 1993.

RIPON MINSTER
NORTH YORKSHIRE

ABOVE: Bishop Longley (right) on the choir screen with, on the left, King James I, who re-established the chapter in 1604. These colourful statues were made and placed into the niches only in 1947.

n 1836, for the first time in three centuries, a new diocese was created in England. This was in North Yorkshire, and its new cathedral was established at the very ancient church of Ripon Minster. The first bishop was C. T. Longley, and he remained for 20 years before moving on to become bishop of Durham and then successively archbishop of York and Canterbury (he appears as a rather strange modern sculpted figure at the right end of the choir screen). Ripon Minster was already a fine medieval building at this time, and had, like the other minsters at Beverley and Southwell, long been associated with the archbishops of York.

Beneath the crossing of this church there survives intact a remarkable, late 7th-century crypt, which was once part of a cathedral church created by St Wilfrid. There is a similar but slightly larger crypt, also created by St Wilfrid, under the nave of Hexham Abbey, but neither of these two places remained a cathedral for long.

A transitional masterpiece

The earliest part of the present building is the early Norman apse and adjoining south wall on the south-east side. Soon after he became archbishop of York in 1154, however, Roger of Pont-l'Evêque gave the huge sum of £1,000 for the construction of a very large new church. This remarkable edifice survives today in the north and south transepts and in the western part of the aisled choir. Unfortunately, the south-east side of the central crossing tower collapsed in about 1450, but the north and west sides of the tower still have their original masonry. The arcades in the western part of the choir show that the new church of Archbishop Roger was remarkably advanced for its time, and Ripon is now one of the most interesting places in England to study 'Transitional' architecture of the late 12th century. The nave in this new church was very wide, but had no aisles, and parts of the walls of the east and west ends of the

RIGHT: This carved misericord depicting a rabbit disappearing down a hole possibly inspired Lewis Carroll's *Alice's Adventures in Wonderland*. Carroll's father, the Revd Charles Dodgson, was a canon of Ripon Minster, so Carroll would have been well-acquainted with these carvings in the choir.

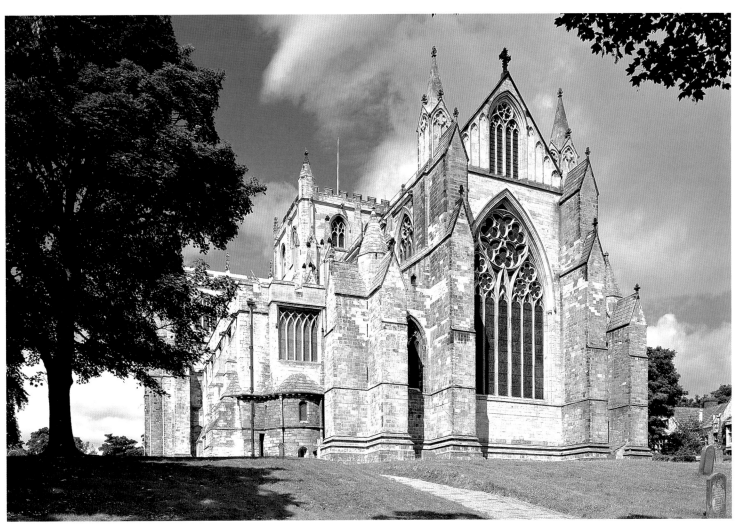

ABOVE: The view of the cathedral from the south-east shows the Norman apse on the left and the magnificent Decorated east window, which dates from the very late 13th century.

RIGHT: The exit passage to the 7th-century crypt. St Wilfrid's crypt is a quite exceptional architectural survival, being, along with that in Hexham Abbey in Northumberland, one of only two very early crypts in England.

original nave can still be seen. In the 1230s another archbishop, Walter de Gray, who also built the magnificent transepts at York Minster, added the fine twin towers to the west end of the nave. Then, at the end of the 13th century, after a partial collapse, the east end of the church was completely rebuilt around a new shrine to St Wilfrid. The east window now contains a magnificent example of Geometrical tracery, which is transitional into the new 'Decorated' style. At about this time three timber and lead spires were added to the towers on the building. All were sadly destroyed in the 17th century.

After the 1450 collapse of the crossing tower, work was slowly put in hand to rebuild the destroyed south-east side of the tower. The breaks between the late 12th and the late 15th century masonry can be seen clearly when looking up into the tower. The final phase of building work, which is equally remarkable, took place mostly in the early years of Henry VIII's reign. This phase saw the complete rebuilding of the nave with, for the first time,

aisles. This work was finished in 1528, though the present aisle vaults and timber roof of the nave were put in as part of Sir George Gilbert Scott's great restoration of 1862–70.

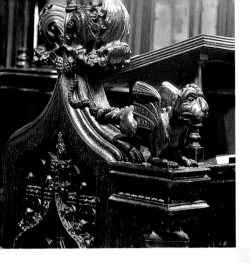

MANCHESTER
GREATER MANCHESTER

ABOVE: It is likely that the craftsmen of c. 1500 who carved the remarkable detail on this bench end in the choir at Manchester Cathedral also worked at Ripon Cathedral and Beverley Minster.

n the northern side of the vast, modern city of Manchester, and close to the River Irwell, is the large collegiate church of St Mary, St Denys and St George. This church became a cathedral in 1847, at a time when the population, which was already about 200,000, was expanding rapidly. The building had become a very wide parish church in the 15th century, with double aisles added to the nave (the outer 'aisles' contained six chantry chapels). To the north was a series of college buildings – the new college of priests was set up in 1421 – which now house the famous Chetham's School of Music and the school for the cathedral choristers. The buildings were turned into a new hospital and school in the 17th century by Humphrey Chetham, and there is a fine statue of him in the nave.

In 1840 the warden and fellows of the old college were turned into a dean and chapter, and seven years later the new diocese was created and

RIGHT: The 1892 south porch was designed by Basil Champneys, while the 130-foot-high west tower behind was rebuilt in 1867.

a bishop's throne was put in the church. In contrast with many other newly created northern cathedrals no large new eastern arm was constructed (there was no available space east of the church in which to put it), but considerable new building work was carried out, starting with the rebuilding of the large west tower (130 feet high) from 1864. At the end of the 19th century and in the earlier 20th, the south-west side of the nave was rebuilt with a new porch, together with many other ancillary buildings to the south-east (vestries, library, choir school, etc.). A new grand porch and western block were also added in 1897, beyond the west tower on the road frontage, to mark Queen Victoria's Diamond Jubilee.

Regrettably the north-east side of the cathedral was badly damaged by bombs in 1940, and the eastern Lady chapel was completely rebuilt after the war, as was the north-east Derby chapel (now the regimental chapel); its east window is now the striking 'fire window', so called because of its vibrant colouration.

BELOW: This impressive monument to Humphrey Chetham, who founded the hospital and school that adjoins the cathedral, can be found in the north-west corner of the cathedral.

At the heart of the cathedral, however, are still some very fine late medieval or early Tudor remains, including the superbly carved choir-stalls, screens and roof. The misericords are particularly noteworthy, with small secular scenes full of interest. Despite much 19th- and 20th-century restoration, the woodwork of the cathedral is exceptional, though one wishes that the interior of the building was not quite so dark.

BELOW: The choir has a wonderful set of 30 canopied stalls, each of which is lit on major feast days by the fine candelabra that hang in the choir.

BIRMINGHAM
ROMAN CATHOLIC
WEST MIDLANDS

DEDICATION

• Metropolitan Cathedral of St Chad

HISTORY

• First church built here in 1808

• Church of St Chad built 1839–41

• Twin spires completed in 1856

• Creation of diocese in 1850 and archdiocese in 1911

• Addition of chapel of St Edward the Confessor in 1933

• Created a 'Minor Basilica' by Pope Pius XII in 1941

OF SPECIAL INTEREST

• Sixteenth-century Flemish pulpit

• Fifteenth-century stalls

• A. W. N. Pugin's high altar and canopy in the sanctuary (with casket containing the relics of St Chad)

• The Immaculate Conception window (1868) by John Hardman

ABOVE: Birmingham became a cathedral in 1850, 11 years after building work began. The later chapel of St Edward is on the right.

his tall brick building in the medieval north German (Baltic) style was built to A. W. N. Pugin's designs between 1839 and 1841, though one of the western towers and its spire was not completed until 1856.

When first put up, this church (of St Chad) was in the run-down gunmakers' quarter of Birmingham, and the steep slope on the north-west side of the church fell away to a canal wharf. Unfortunately, all of this (as well as the house Pugin designed for the bishop—an archbishop from 1911) was levelled in the 1960s, and the cathedral was left in isolation beside a major new inner ring-road scheme (St Chad's Circus) to the north of Snow Hill station. Subsequently, many tall office blocks were built in the surrounding area. While this was going on, the interior of the church was damaged in 1967, when Pugin's fine Rood screen and Rood were removed and the walls were painted cream (some of this paint is now peeling off, to reveal traces of the original scheme).

In spite of all this, the interior of the cathedral is a very fine architectural space, with the tall piers in the nave reaching up to the high, painted timber roof. Some of Pugin's colour has been restored, and the sanctuary, behind the opened-up crossing (with its modern altar), still contains many fine fittings, including some good 15th-century canons' stalls from Cologne and Pugin's richly decorated high altar under its wooden canopy, painted in red and gold. There is also much fine glass in the church, and a beautiful early 16th-century wooden pulpit from Louvain. One later addition is the chapel of St Edward, designed by S. Pugin Powell in 1931–3.

LEFT: The modern high altar replaced A. W. N. Pugin's wonderful gilded and painted Rood screen. The Lady chapel is just to the left of the nave.

CLIFTON

ROMAN CATHOLIC

BRISTOL

his very striking and completely modern cathedral of saints Peter and Paul was commissioned and designed in 1965, and then built in two and a half years (1970–73) on a new site in Clifton. It replaced a rather sad pro-cathedral of the Apostles in Bristol, which had been started in 1834 and never finished. The original church was to have been a huge Corinthian temple, but the money ran out when only the first part had been built. Then in 1847–8 it was redesigned with an Italian Romanesque front, and became the pro-cathedral in 1850; the first part of the scheme was finally finished in 1876. A tall tower (200 feet high) was planned, but nothing further was built.

In the early 1960s a major renovation and reordering were considered by the bishop, but the cost was too high. Instead, with the help of local businessmen, the completely new cathedral was built at an overall cost of £800,000. This building, uncompromisingly made of concrete, is on a hexagonal plan with an equilateral triangle as the basis for all its proportions. At the centre is the high altar, beneath a pyramid-like lantern surmounted by a concrete flèche. There is then an uninterrupted space for nearly 1,000 people to the south, with more peripheral sites for the Lady chapel and Blessed Sacrament chapel. Major doors, called St Peter's and St Paul's doors, lead out to bridges (known as atria) over the screened car-parks beneath. All in all, Clifton is a most interesting 1960s concept.

ABOVE RIGHT: The lantern and flèche combine to create a highly modern design for Clifton Roman Catholic Cathedral, designed by F. S. Jennett, R. Weeks and A. Poremba of the Percy Thomas Partnership.

BELOW: Looking north across the cathedral with the baptistery in the distance.

DEDICATION

- Cathedral Church of St Peter and St Paul

HISTORY

- Church of the Apostles in Bristol became a pro-cathedral in 1850
- New cathedral built at Clifton 1970–73
- Consecration of the cathedral on 29 June 1973

OF SPECIAL INTEREST

- Stone font by Simon Verity
- Narthex windows by Henry Haig (made from over 800 pieces of coloured glass)
- Stations of the Cross in carved concrete by William Mitchell

LIVERPOOL

ROMAN CATHOLIC

MERSEYSIDE

DEDICATION

• Metropolitan Cathedral of Christ the King

HISTORY

• Diocese of Liverpool founded in 1850

• Becomes a Metropolitan cathedral (with an archbishop) in 1911

• Sir Edwin Lutyens designs huge new 'Byzantine' cathedral in 1930 (only podium and vast crypt built)

• New competition for a 'cheaper' cathedral 1959–60

• Sir Frederick Gibberd's circular cathedral built 1962–7

• Visit of Pope John Paul II in 1982

OF SPECIAL INTEREST

• Lutyens's crypt

• The vast open space around the high altar

• Glass in lantern by John Piper and Patrick Reyntiens

ABOVE: The eighth Station of the Cross.

BELOW: The vast open centre is dominated by the elevated high altar.

iverpool is the most stark and modern cathedral in England, and stands not far from the huge Anglican cathedral in this great city and sea port. It was rapidly built (1962–7) in concrete as a great circular 'tent', at a time when British architecture was sadly at a low point. Nevertheless, the vast circular space inside the cathedral, 200 feet in diameter, makes an excellent setting for the new liturgies of the Roman church – for example the great High Mass for the Pope in 1982. The impressive 19-ton white marble altar at the centre of the structure is lit from above by the huge lantern that dominates the outside of the building. The lantern, which is crowned by spiky 'pinnacles', is filled with a mass of modern coloured glass. Round the edge of the structure, in the space between the slanting 'tent poles', are the doors and a series of small chapels of different shapes, including a small circular baptistery. Above the main door is a large sloping slab in which are hung the bells; it cannot really be called a campanile. What a contrast to the elegant structure at Westminster Cathedral!

ABOVE: The great tent that is Liverpool's Roman Catholic cathedral, with its vast 16-sided lantern with spiky pinnacles, was designed by Sir Frederick Gibberd in 1959.

This structure sits on the southern end of a great rectangular podium, within which is the very large crypt for an immense cathedral, designed by Sir Edwin Lutyens in 1930 to be the largest in the world. This cathedral was to be 680 feet long and to have a dome 168 feet in diameter and 510 feet high – even larger than the dome of St Peter's in Rome. Work stopped in 1939, and was sadly never continued, unlike the work on Liverpool's Anglican cathedral, which is located just down the road from this cathedral. In 1960 a competition for the design of the new cathedral was won by Sir Frederick Gibberd – there were 298 entries – and his vast steel and concrete structure was built upon Lutyens's podium.

NEWCASTLE UPON TYNE
ROMAN CATHOLIC
TYNE & WEAR

ABOVE: Hansom's prominent tower and spire make Newcastle upon Tyne's Roman Catholic cathedral a distinctive landmark. A. W. N. Pugin's east end is also just visible above the trees.

his cathedral stands just to the north-west of the central station, and its very tall, thin, 222-foot high spire stands out clearly in the city centre. The church was built in 1844 by A. W. N. Pugin, and though he intended it to have a spire, this was never built. The present spire was designed by Joseph A. Hansom, who also put up tall spires at such places as Plymouth Cathedral. Hansom's fine structure here was erected in the 1860s, just after the church was raised to cathedral status for the diocese of Hexham and Newcastle; the first cathedral after 1850 was at Hexham.

Pugin's church, which runs north-west to south-east alongside a street, has triple gables at either end with large windows under each gable, each containing Decorated-style tracery. The aisles have three-light windows, with no clerestory to the nave. Inside the building, the arcades and general proportions are rather plain. The main entrance, on the north-west, is close to the polygonal baptistery, added to the cathedral in 1902.

RIGHT: The Blessed Sacrament chapel sits in the south-east corner of the cathedral. The fine stained glass of the east window was made by William Wailes to A. W. N. Pugin's designs.

NORTHAMPTON

ROMAN CATHOLIC

NORTHAMPTONSHIRE

ABOVE RIGHT: The new 1950s brick eastern arm was designed by Albert Herbert.

he relatively small and unassuming cathedral at Northampton has developed in a piecemeal way. A chapel was first built here, dedicated to St Andrew, in 1825. Then in 1844, with the worshipping population increasing after the Catholic Emancipation Act, a new collegiate chapel of St Felix was built beside the earlier chapel, to a design by A. W. N. Pugin. This became the first cathedral in 1850, and a large aisled nave was added to it by Pugin's son, E. W. Pugin, in 1864. At the west end of the aisled nave, a small polygonal sanctuary was added, which turned the whole building round to face west. This was now the cathedral church of Our Lady and St Thomas (Becket), and E. W. Pugin's design, with its straight pews (in the aisles as well as the nave) is still intact, though a west door was later cut through the sanctuary. At the centre of the nave is a brass commemorating Bishop Amherst (died 1883).

The final major change came in 1955 when Bishop Leo Parker demolished the old collegiate chapel of 1844 and laid the foundation for a new brick eastern arm; this material contrasts with the Northampton stone of the earlier work. The new arm had a new crossing tower, shallow transepts and a new eastern chancel flanked by small chapels, and was completed in 1959. The whole church, with its 1864 nave, was then turned round to face east again. The altar was brought forward to the crossing, and in 1998 another reordering was carried out, with a colourful triptych by Stephen Foster added to the east wall to replace the high altar and reredos.

LEFT: The cathedral's chancel is dominated by two relatively recent additions – the painted ceiling of 1959 and the triptych of 1998 by Stephen Foster.

DEDICATION

- Cathedral Church of Our Lady and of St Thomas

HISTORY

- The first chapel of St Andrew was built in 1825
- Collegiate chapel of St Felix added in 1844
- Diocese of Northampton (including East Anglia) created in 1850
- New aisled nave (and western sanctuary) added to collegiate chapel in 1864
- New eastern arm built 1955–9
- Major reordering in 1998

OF SPECIAL INTEREST

- Brass, in nave, for Bishop Francis Amherst (1883)
- Timber roof, with iron ties, in nave (1864)
- Stained glass windows in old 1864 sanctuary, with illustrations of Northampton's medieval buildings carefully delineated in the central bottom lights

NOTTINGHAM
ROMAN CATHOLIC
NOTTINGHAMSHIRE

DEDICATION

• Cathedral Church of St Barnabas

HISTORY

• New church of St Barnabas built 1841–4

• Destructive restoration of interior from 1962

• Major reordering and redecoration in 1993

OF SPECIAL INTEREST

• The surviving, restored internal wall-decoration by A. W. N. Pugin, especially in the Blessed Sacrament chapel

• Fine stained glass designed by A. W. N. Pugin and made by William Wailes

ABOVE: The cleaning of the building sadly disposed of much of the wonderful colours introduced to the interior by A. W. N. Pugin.

his fine building just to the north-west of the historic city of Nottingham, is dedicated to St Barnabas, and was built in 1841–4 to the designs of A. W. N. Pugin. It is 190 feet long, in the Early English (lancet) style, and has a very full plan with an aisled nave and north and south porches; transepts with chapels; an aisled presbytery and an ambulatory with eastern chapels, including a central Lady chapel. Over the crossing is a prominent tower and spire 150 feet high, which draws the building together. The whole of the exterior has recently been cleaned.

Inside the cathedral there has been a fair amount of restoration, cleaning and relighting (particularly in 1993), and this has given the cathedral a colourful and clean interior, showing off some striking tiled floors. However, much of Pugin's original interior fittings and furnishings have been removed or altered, including his Rood screen. The Rood itself still hangs at the entrance to the presbytery. Despite this Nottingham still retains much more colour than many 19th-century Roman Catholic cathedrals, such as Birmingham or Salford, and the 1993 restoration has done much to enhance the building. The conservation and restoration of the Blessed Sacrament chapel, to the east of the south transept, has been a triumph (see page 103), and once more it is possible get some idea of Pugin's rich use of colour in his churches. Sadly, it is probably too much to hope that the old sanctuary, now called the retro-choir, will one day be redecorated to its original colour scheme.

LEFT: Since being cleaned in 1985 the fine stonework of A. W. N. Pugin's elaborate cathedral is shown off to much better advantage.

PLYMOUTH
ROMAN CATHOLIC
DEVON

ABOVE RIGHT: The exceptionally splendid tower and spire by Joseph Hansom are striking features in the rather drab streets of this area of Plymouth.

RIGHT: The new high altar at the crossing sits upon an octagonal base; the old sanctuary is beyond the altar.

he diocese of Plymouth was created in 1850, and a new cathedral of St Mary and St Boniface was designed and built for Bishop William Vaughan (1814–1902), the first bishop, in 1856–8. The design was by the brothers Joseph Aloysius and Charles Francis Hansom, with Charles probably doing most of the initial design. The site, off Cecil Street, on a hillside on the north-west side of Plymouth, is rather restricted, though a cruciform plan for the cathedral was achieved. In 1866 a very tall thin spire, 205 feet high, was added to the north-west tower. This was designed by Joseph Hansom, and it now dominates this part of the city.

The rather sparse interior of the building, with thin granite octagonal columns and pairs of lancets, was restored in 1920–27 by F. A. Walters. He added much colour to the Blessed Sacrament chapel, where there is a brass commemorating Bishop Vaughan with a recumbent figure. Further restoration was carried out in 1956–7 and again more recently, and the cathedral now has a clean and much more striking interior.

DEDICATION

- Cathedral of St Mary and St Boniface

HISTORY

- Creation of new diocese for Cornwall, Devon and Dorset in 1850
- New cathedral built 1856–8
- Very tall thin spire added in 1866
- Restoration of cathedral by F. A. Walters 1920–27
- Second restoration by Hugh Bankart 1956–7

OF SPECIAL INTEREST

- Late Victorian stained glass by John Hardman
- Brass to Bishop William Vaughan (1902) by Hardman & Co.
- Blessed Sacrament chapel in south transept

SALFORD

ROMAN CATHOLIC

GREATER MANCHESTER

DEDICATION

- Cathedral Church of St John the Evangelist

HISTORY

- New church for Salford built 1844–8
- Diocese of Salford created in 1850
- Eastern arm furnished 1853–5
- Reordering in 1972

OF SPECIAL INTEREST

- Fine stained glass in eastern arm
- Blessed Sacrament chapel in the south transept (1884)
- Tomb of Bishop Sharples in the north transept (1850)

ABOVE: Fine mid-19th-century stained glass and carving dominate the chancel. The beautiful flowing tracery of the east window was copied from Selby Abbey in 1859.

RIGHT: The proportions of Matthew Hadfield's Decorated Gothic cathedral are particularly satisfying.

ess than a mile to the west of the Anglican cathedral in central Manchester is the large Roman Catholic cathedral in Salford. Whereas central Manchester and the Anglican cathedral are surrounded by substantial, shiny new buildings, Salford Cathedral is in an area that is still largely derelict. The splendid great church, with its tall spire, built in 1844–8, therefore stands out.

The design, by Matthew Hadfield, is based on three medieval churches: Selby, Newark and Howden. The inside of the building is in the early 14th-century Gothic style, and is particularly spacious, with a large aisled nave and presbytery and two big transepts. There is much fine carved stonework, particularly in the presbytery, but sadly most of the interior has been stripped of its earlier furnishings, which were installed in 1853–5, and the walls have been mainly painted white. Only P. P. Pugin's (third son of A.W. N. Pugin) 1884 fittings, in the south transept – the Blessed Sacrament chapel – survive.

As is usual nowadays, there is a new main altar under the crossing, and the old choir and sanctuary have been stripped bare. The one great survival from the earlier cathedral is the fine stained glass, and the east window still contains many fine coloured figures of saints. By contrast, the large west window now contains new glass, in a modern style, which is rather pale in appearance. Here is a cathedral that is crying out for strong new colours.

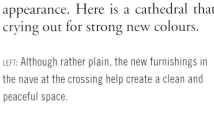

LEFT: Although rather plain, the new furnishings in the nave at the crossing help create a clean and peaceful space.

SHREWSBURY

ROMAN CATHOLIC

SHROPSHIRE

ABOVE RIGHT: The nave of Shrewsbury's Roman Catholic cathedral stands prominently above the old city walls.

ust one year after the restoration of the Hierarchy by Pope Pius IX, James Brown was consecrated bishop in the new Southwark Cathedral. Later in 1851, the earl of Shrewsbury offered to build a new cathedral for Bishop Brown, with A. W. N. Pugin as architect. Land was bought just inside the southern city walls in 1852, but unfortunately both Pugin and the earl died soon afterwards. Luckily the new earl, who was only 20 years old, agreed to finance the work, and Pugin's son, Edward, was able to complete his father's designs and oversee the construction from 1853 to 1856. E. W. Pugin's design had to be considerably modified because of difficult geological conditions, and the projected tall tower and spire were abandoned. The earl asked that the church be given the unusual dedication to 'Our Lady Help of Christians and St Peter of Alcantara'; tragically he died, aged only 23, just two months before the cathedral was opened on 29 October 1856 in the presence of Cardinal Wiseman.

The cathedral today looks much as it did when completed nearly 150 years ago, though a bigger centre porch was added in 1907. It has a large aisled nave with a separate chancel and side chapels. E. W. Pugin's fine high altar and reredos, made of Caen stone, were superseded by a new altar in 1984–5, and sadly the pulpit and altar rails have gone. Redecoration in the 1950s also saw the earlier wall decoration painted out. Much good stained glass, which remains, was added in the later 19th century. The fine Blessed Sacrament chapel was added in 1901, and it now contains the fine Victorian Gothic tabernacle, which was previously located in the centre of the reredos above the high altar.

DEDICATION
- Cathedral Church of Our Lady Help of Christians and St Peter of Alcantara

HISTORY
- Diocese of Shrewsbury created in 1850
- New cathedral built by E. W. Pugin 1853–6
- Blessed Sacrament chapel built in 1901
- New west porch added in 1907
- Major reordering in 1984

OF SPECIAL INTEREST
- Blessed Sacrament chapel (formerly St Winifred's chapel)
- Many good later Victorian and early 20th-century furnishings and stained glass

LEFT: An altar from 1985 sits at the east end of the nave, while behind it is the 1885 hanging Rood cross and the old sanctuary. E. W. Pugin's font of 1856 is in the foreground.

SOUTHWARK

ROMAN CATHOLIC

LONDON

DEDICATION

- Metropolitan Cathedral of St George

HISTORY

- New church built by A. W. N. Pugin 1840–48
- Cardinal Wiseman enthroned here as first Archbishop of Westminster in 1850
- Bombed and gutted by fire on 16 April 1941
- Church rebuilt 1953–8
- New Lady chapel added in 1963, and baptistery in 1966
- Visited by Pope John Paul II in 1982

OF SPECIAL INTEREST

- The Blessed Sacrament Chapel, with A. W. N. Pugin's furnishings
- The Petre (1848–9) and Knill (1857) chantry chapels
- Monument to Provost Thomas Doyle (d. 1879), in north aisle

ABOVE: The main entrance and uncompleted south tower on Lambeth Road. The new baptistery is behind the tower on the right.

his little-known building is situated less than a mile due east of the Houses of Parliament on a site that is surrounded by major roads and lies opposite the Imperial War Museum. Just down the road is the archbishop of Canterbury's palace at Lambeth, but it was at St George's that the first archbishop of Westminster, Cardinal Wiseman, was enthroned in 1850, after Pope Pius IX had restored the English Hierarchy.

The site within the previously open St George's Fields was first purchased in 1839, and A. W. N. Pugin was commissioned to produce a design for a major new Gothic church. Unfortunately, the money was not available, and he had to produce a much smaller design, which was built in 1840–48. This was his most important church in London, but it was heavily criticized by John Ruskin and others.

Sadly, the building was bombed and burnt out in April 1941, and now all that remains of Pugin's church are the east end, the long brick aisle walls and the lowest part of the west tower; Pugin's great steeple has never been built. Between 1953 and 1958 the church was rebuilt by Romilly Craze, and he tried to give the building a grander appearance

with a clerestory and stone vaults. The interesting aisle vaults were made (with flying ribs like Bristol Cathedral), but the nave vaults were never constructed, and the transverse arches, panelled ceiling and strange clerestory windows have an unsettling effect. The two chantry chapels, by Pugin and his son, Edward, for the Petre and Knill families respectively, are now perhaps the most interesting interior features. It is remarkable that A. W. N. Pugin's original furnishings have survived in the Blessed Sacrament chapel.

LEFT: The Knill chantry chapel was designed in 1857 by E. W. Pugin, whose father married his third wife, Jane Knill, at the church in 1848.

WESTMINSTER

ROMAN CATHOLIC

LONDON

his splendid building was completed exactly a century ago, and it is certainly the finest Roman Catholic cathedral in England. Since the cleaning of the exterior and the rebuilding of neighbouring Victoria Street area 25 years ago, the external views of the cathedral from the north have been greatly enhanced, and it was a stroke of genius to add a great Italianate campanile to one side of the building, This 285-foot-high brick structure with stone stripes is reminiscent of Siena Cathedral's bell-tower, and forms one of the few really good landmarks in this part of London.

ABOVE RIGHT: The chapel of St Patrick commemorates the 50,000 Irish soldiers who died in the First World War. Many types of Irish marble were used in its decoration.

RIGHT: The campanile and main entrance make a striking scene from the square off Victoria Street, reminiscent of Italian and Spanish church squares. This elegant structure, with its huge 'minaret', could also be mistaken for a mosque. It is interesting to note that the architect J. F. Bentley (1839–1902) initially proposed having two towers.

DEDICATION

• Metropolitan Cathedral of the Most Precious Blood, St Mary, St Joseph and St Peter

HISTORY

• The most important Roman Catholic cathedral in England and the seat of the archbishop of Westminster
• Built to J. F. Bentley's designs 1895–1903
• Much internal decoration (mosaics and marble wall veneering, etc.) added in the 20th century
• Burial place of many cardinals, the archbishops of Westminster
• Visited by Pope John Paul II in 1982

OF SPECIAL INTEREST

• External brickwork and great bell-tower
• *Stations of the Cross* by Eric Gill (1913–18)
• Much exceptional decoration in the side chapels
• Large baldacchino over the high altar
• Shrine of St John Southworth (and glass sarcophagus) in the chapel of St George

ABOVE: The recent grave of Cardinal Basil Hume lies in the chapel of St Gregory. Cardinal Hume, who died on 17 June 1999, was the ninth archbishop of Westminster.

LEFT: Looking up the nave gives an excellent view of the baldacchino over the high altar, to the left of which sits the *cathedra* – a copy of the Pope's *cathedra* in St John Lateran in Rome.

The cathedral was designed for Cardinal Vaughan by J. F. Bentley and was rapidly built (1895–1903) using Justinian's great church of the Holy Wisdom (St Sophia) in Constantinople and San Vitale at Ravenna as its principal models. Looking up inside the building a series of very black arches and domes (in fact, dirty brickwork) are visible, and one day these, like some of the side chapels, may be covered in mosaic work. The side walls, or brick piers, have been covered in magnificent marble veneering over the last century. This, and the marble and porphyry flooring, give the areas on either side of the nave a wonderful and dramatic colouring which is enhanced by Eric Gill's very fine panels of the Stations of the Cross put in during the First World War. At the far end of the nave is the sanctuary with a monumental marble baldacchino over the high altar. Beside it is the *cathedra*, a copy of the Pope's own throne in St John Lateran, Rome.

TRURO
CORNWALL

ABOVE RIGHT: This was once the south aisle of the old parish church of St Mary's, which stood here before the new cathedral was built. The aisle still serves as the parish church for the city centre.

here had been a cathedral for the Cornish at St Germans between 931 and 1043, but after this date the see was amalgamated with Devon. It was not until 1876 that a new diocese for the county, based on Truro, was created. Soon afterwards a remarkable man, Edward White Benson, was made the first bishop, and he was determined to have a brand new cathedral in Truro to replace the dilapidated parish church of St Mary and in spite of the fact that Cornwall was, at this time, a very poor county. In 1877 a committee was formed and seven prominent architects were invited to submit designs, and it is clear that the brief was to include three tall spires – a central spire and two western ones. This was, no doubt, because the new bishop had previously been chancellor of Lincoln, and was a lover of great Gothic buildings. After much discussion, the bishop and committee appointed the 60-year-old J. L. Pearson, who was architect, or 'surveyor', at Lincoln and was soon also to take on Westminster Abbey. His designs were ready by 1879, and on 20 May 1880 a great foundation ceremony was held that was as much masonic as it was Christian. The Prince of Wales (later Edward VII) laid foundation stones on the north-east side and for a pillar in the proposed nave. Work then began on demolishing all of the old parish church except for the fine early 16th-century south aisle.

A Norman legacy

Pearson very cleverly designed his 275-foot-long cathedral on the sloping site in the centre of Truro with an already existing small square, called High Cross, on the west. His inspiration was not really Lincoln, but the great churches of Normandy: Coutances Cathedral can be seen as having a strong influence on the overall shape of the three tall towers and spires. The new cathedral was to have an aisled nave and choir separated by the great crossing tower, as well as shallow aisled transepts.

RIGHT: The elaborately carved 'Phillpott's' south porch was named after Henry Phillpott, bishop of Exeter (1830–69). Phillpott paved the way for the recreation of the Cornish diocese. The decorated porch also contains a statue of its architect, J. L. Pearson.

The foundations of the eastern arm were started first, and a crypt was made under the eastern end, where the ground fell away. The whole of the eastern arm, with the transepts, crossing and an unusual circular baptistery, were built in seven years (1880–87), and this part of the building then came into use. Benson had

DEDICATION

• Cathedral Church of St Mary

HISTORY

• Parish church of St Mary consecrated in 1259

• Cornish diocese reconstituted in 1876

• Choir and transepts of new cathedral built 1880–87

• Nave built 1896–1903

• Western towers completed in 1910

• First dean of Truro created in 1960 (before this there was just a rector)

OF SPECIAL INTEREST

• Statue of J. L. Pearson, the cathedral's architect (d. 1897), on the south porch

• The baptistery and font, made of many different types of stone

• Many fine furnishings, including bishop's throne (of teak), choir stalls and Cosmatesque pavements

• Father Willis organ of 1887 (rebuilt 1991)

• Robartes memorial (c. 1614) in north transept

BELOW: View from the southeast, with the old 16th-century St Mary's aisle in the foreground. The 244-foot-high central tower and spire were generously paid for by one man, Hawke Dennis.

moved on to become archbishop of Canterbury in 1883, and the impetus to finish the building only came through the architect's son, Frank, after Pearson's death in 1896.

The nave was completed by 1903, followed by the western towers in 1910, and after 30 years J. L. Pearson's great Gothic design was finally realized, though sadly his plan for a new cloister and chapter house on the north was never completed. The concrete 'chapter house' and 'undercroft' carpark (built in 1967) that now lies on the north is not worthy of Pearson's design, and should be either demolished or completely covered by new work. Apart from this, Truro Cathedral has been a very successful 'Gothic' design that fits well in the town. It is perhaps the most successful new-old design of any cathedral in the 19th or 20th centuries.

ST ALBAN'S ABBEY
HERTFORDSHIRE

ABOVE RIGHT: The wonderful reredos behind the high altar – a gift from Abbot William Wallingford (1476–1484) – cost 100 marks.

BELOW LEFT & RIGHT: Reused Roman bricks and Anglo-Saxon baluster shafts in the triforium. A 13th-century wall-painting continues, in the 21st century, to decorate a nave pier.

his huge building became a cathedral only in 1877, exactly 800 years after the work on the present building was started by Abbot Paul of Caen. At first sight, however, much of the outside of the building looks Victorian – as indeed it is, because the building was very heavily restored in the 20 years after it became a cathedral and before a dean and chapter were created in 1899. Almost all the restoration work was undertaken and funded by Sir Edmund Beckett (later Lord Grimthorpe), an immensely wealthy railway lawyer and amateur architect. Beckett, who was perhaps most famous for having designed Big Ben, the clock and great bell for the new Palace of Westminster, was an autocrat who was able to do what he liked at St Alban's, because he was paying for it all. Unfortunately this means that much of the exterior of the building now bears little resemblance to the earlier building; this is particularly the case in the transept façades and on the west front, where the mechanically cut Ketton and Ancaster stone shows that this is only a poor late Victorian design.

Roman foundations

Remarkably, large amounts of the masonry of the original great church, which was built for a huge and wealthy Benedictine abbey and was started in 1077, came from the ruins of the Roman city of Verulamium, which lies just to the south-west of the abbey. Much

DEDICATION
- Cathedral and Abbey Church of St Alban

HISTORY
- Probable site of the martyrdom of St Alban in the 3rd century AD
- Site of later Anglo-Saxon abbey
- Present great church started by Abbot Paul (a nephew of Archbishop Lanfranc) in 1077
- The abbot became the premier abbot of England in 1154
- Nave extended to 13 bays in 1195
- New shrine of St Alban built in 1308
- New diocese created in 1877
- Dean and chapter created in 1899

OF SPECIAL INTEREST
- Newly reconstructed shrine (1991–3) with timber 'watching loft' to the north (1413–29)
- Roman brick crossing tower
- Wall-paintings in the nave
- Early 14th-century Lady chapel
- Chantry chapel (with fine iron grill) for Humphrey, Duke of Gloucester (1447)
- High altar reredos of the 1480s (similar to that in Winchester Cathedral)

ABOVE The view of the cathedral from the south-west clearly shows the Roman brick central tower – a fine example of early architectural salvage from the nearby Roman town. Grimthorpe's rebuilt transept is to its right. The abbey cloister would originally have been in the foreground of this view.

Roman brick is still visible externally, especially in the tower. The Roman brick was originally covered in white plaster, and inside the building much of this plaster, decorated with wall-paintings, still survives.

Early in the 12th century a fine new white limestone (a form of hard chalk) was discovered not far away at Totternhoe, and this stone, which could be easily cut, is used for most of the later medieval work in the cathedral. This can best be seen in the enlarged eastern arm and Lady chapel, and in the south side of the nave,

which had to be rebuilt after a collapse in 1323.

At the heart of the east end of the cathedral is the shrine of St Alban, an early Christian martyr from late Roman Britain whose earlier shrine throughout the Anglo-Saxon period was in a much smaller building nearby. This shrine was built in 1302–8 and then smashed in 1539. It was reconstructed in 1872, but very recently a fine new reconstruction of the fragments has taken place, making it one of the finest 'modern' shrines in any English cathedral (see page 11).

LEEDS

ROMAN CATHOLIC

WEST YORKSHIRE

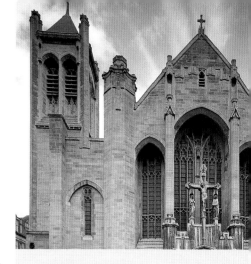

I n 1878 the earlier diocese of Beverley (of 1850) was divided into two – Middlesbrough and Leeds – and a church of St Anne, which had been built in 1836–8 in the town centre, became the cathedral of the new diocese. This church was compulsorily purchased, and then demolished in 1900, and the city corporation subsequently gave the diocese some land nearby on the corner of Cookridge Street and Great George Street. A London architect, John Henry Eastwood (1843–1913), who was born near Leeds, was chosen, and he and his assistant, Sydney Kyffin Greenslade (1866–1955), produced a very fine design to fit the street-corner site, with a large tower on the north.

On the south-west is a porch leading to a nave with narrow aisles and a series of side chapels. The new building, which was put up between 1901 and 1904, is in the late Gothic style of the Arts and Crafts Movement, with a boldly painted barrel-vaulted roof. A major restoration project was started in 1985 under the present architect, Donald Buttress, and this has seen the grimy exterior cleaned and repaired, and the original iron railings around the church put back. Internal work was also carried out.

ABOVE RIGHT: Detail of John Henry Eastwood's bell-tower and the upper part of the west front, which was cleaned in 1987.

RIGHT: The Edwardian Arts and Crafts interior has been cleaned and restored in recent years. On the left of the picture the bishop's throne, or *cathedra*, is visible

DEDICATION

- Cathedral Church of St Anne

HISTORY

- St Anne's church (built 1836–8) becomes a cathedral in 1878
- Compulsory purchase and demolition of the cathedral in 1900
- New cathedral built 1901–4
- Major restoration in 1985

OF SPECIAL INTEREST

- Painted reredoses by A. W. N. Pugin, made in 1842 for the earlier church
- Fine Arts and Crafts Gothic barrel-vaulted nave

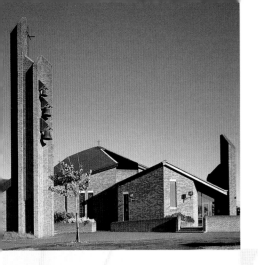

MIDDLESBROUGH
ROMAN CATHOLIC
NORTH YORKSHIRE

DEDICATION

- St Mary's Cathedral

HISTORY

- Church of St Mary in Middlesbrough built 1876–8
- New diocese of Middlesbrough (for the North and East Ridings of Yorkshire) created in 1878
- New cathedral built at Coulby Newham 1985–7

OF SPECIAL INTEREST

- New furnishings and fittings, including painted reredos and Portland stone altar, bishop's chair and *ambo*
- Campanile and three external bells

ABOVE: One of England's most speedily constructed cathedrals: Middlesbrough's redbrick cathedral, cathedral house and campanile were built in just two years.

RIGHT: The interior of Middlesbrough Cathedral is dominated by R. W. Brumby's painted reredos, which stands behind the bishop's chair and large Portland stone high altar.

he diocese of Middlesbrough was formed out of the 1850 diocese of Beverley in 1878. The new cathedral was built from 1876 to 1878 in Sussex Street, Middlesbrough, by the architect George Goldie. Regrettably this building was allowed to deteriorate in the 1980s, after the cathedral was moved to a completely new site, which was first discussed in 1976; the original cathedral has since been destroyed after a sad final decade.

The completely new cathedral is at Coulby Newham, five miles south of the old city-centre site, in a rapidly developing new town. Appropriately, the new cathedral is next to a large new shopping centre, car-park and bus terminal, on an open site with plenty of room for ancillary buildings. The new design, by Frank Swainston (who died in 1982) and his assistant Peter Fenton, was completed in the early 1980s, and the foundation stone was laid in November 1985. The building was finished in two years, and in form it can be roughly compared with Clifton Cathedral, another church that was created for the liturgical changes of the Second Vatican Council. This cathedral is, however, a 1980s structure, so concrete has given way to a steel frame with brick facings and slate roofs. The large Portland stone altar at the centre is flanked by the *ambo* (lectern) and bishop's chair, and all of these are clearly visible to the congregation which is spread out in three directions. Externally, the most striking feature is the 60-foot-high brick campanile with three bells hanging on one side of it.

LIVERPOOL

MERSEYSIDE

he diocese of Liverpool was created in 1880, after the Bishoprics' Act of 1878 made it independent of Chester. For many years the now-demolished church of St Peter in Liverpool, which dated from 1699, acted as a 'provisional' cathedral, but then in 1904 the foundation stone was laid for a vast new 20th-century cathedral on a completely new site. The site chosen was a rock ridge above an old quarry, called St James Mount, which ran north–south (hence the cathedral also had to be built north–south) and looked down on the docks of the River Mersey.

This vast cathedral, one of the largest in the world, was built in the first three-quarters of the 20th century – it was finally finished in 1978 – and in many ways was already an anachronism when it was started. The architect was Sir Giles Gilbert Scott, a Roman Catholic and the grandson of the famous Sir George Gilbert Scott. In 1903 Giles Gilbert

ABOVE RIGHT: Sited upon the cliffs of an old quarry, Liverpool Cathedral may well have been one of the 20th century's longest building projects: it was begun in 1904, but the last work, which was on the nave (the north-west corner of which is visible here), was finally completed in 1978.

RIGHT: Liverpool's Lady chapel is very different from the rest of the cathedral, as it was designed at the very beginning of the project by Sir Giles Gilbert Scott and his mentor, G. F. Bodley.

DEDICATION

- Cathedral Church of Christ

HISTORY

- Diocese created with pro-cathedral at St Peter's church in 1880
- Foundation for new cathedral laid on St James Mount in 1904
- Consecration of Lady chapel in 1910 (reopened in 1955)
- Choir and southern arm consecrated in 1924
- Central space and transepts completed in 1941
- Final completion of the nave in 1978

OF SPECIAL INTEREST

- The large interior spaces
- Memorial to 20th-century bishops and deans, and to the earl of Derby
- Detailing and furnishings in Lady chapel
- Modern painted glass
- Baptistery with marble font and huge baldacchino

Scott, at the tender age of 22, won a public competition to design a totally new cathedral. He spent a good deal of the rest of his life working on the building, but he sadly died in 1960, 18 years before it was finally finished.

The making of a modern cathedral

A huge foundation stone was laid by King Edward VII in 1904, and for the next six years a large Lady chapel was built, which was to be on the south corner of the new cathedral. For the first stage of the project Sir Giles Gilbert Scott had the eminent architect G. F. Bodley working with him – Bodley had been an assessor at the original competition – and so the elaborate 'Decorated Gothic' of this part of the cathedral is very different from the rest.

Flanking the other corner of the high altar wall was a small, octagonal chapter house, and by 1924 this and the south arm (choir and south transepts) had been built and consecrated. Then came the building of the vast central space under the Vestey tower (named after the Vestey family who paid for its building as a family memorial), which was completed in 1941, after the Blitz and some severe weather had hampered the work. The Lady chapel was reopened, with new stained glass, only in 1955. The extraordinary central space is surrounded by the four transepts, the inner angles of which support the huge 331-foot tower, and was completed in 1949. On either side of the tower, between each of the pairs of transepts, was a monumental porch. The central tower received a colossal peal of 13 bells – the largest, 'Great George', weighs 16½ tons! – and the cathedral itself received one of the world's largest organs.

The nave and west (actually north) porch were not built until after the war, when Scott's design had been modified once again. By comparison with the rest of the building, the nave is a relatively small space, particularly considering that Scott's earlier schemes had a huge six-bay nave, though by 1927 this had already been reduced to three. By 1961 the first part of the nave, with its remarkable bridge, was ready, but it was not until 15 October 1978 that the Queen was able to come to the great service of Dedication and Thanksgiving that marked the end of the whole project.

LEFT: View through the nave bridge to the choir and high altar. This extraordinary cathedral marked the end of an era, and it is still a fine memorial to the Edwardian age before the First World War.

NEWCASTLE UPON TYNE

TYNE & WEAR

ow the most northerly cathedral in England, the see for Northumberland having been created in 1882, the first church here was built at the end of the 11th century, close to the 'New Castle' of Robert Curthose (who built it for his father, William the Conqueror, in 1080). In the early 12th century the church was given to the new priory and cathedral at Carlisle by Henry I. In the 14th and 15th centuries the church became one of the largest parish churches in England, in the middle of a flourishing town.

Despite the stripping of the interior in 1783–5 (a lesser version of what happened at Salisbury Cathedral) and much 19th-century restoration, a great deal survives of the later medieval fabric. The most splendid feature of that fabric is the great west tower, which is surmounted by the finest crown steeple in Britain. It predates that at St Giles, Edinburgh, and was much admired by Sir Christopher Wren, who based his design for the steeple of St Dunstan-in-the-East (in London) on it.

Remarkably, this church almost became a cathedral in 1553, when Parliament passed an act to set up a new bishopric of Newcastle with a dean and chapter. The fiery Protestant reformer John Knox was suggested as the first bishop, but this all quickly came to nothing with the death of Edward VI.

Since the church finally became a cathedral in 1882, no enlargements of the building have been undertaken to make it more 'cathedral-like', though a hall, library and vestry were added on the north-east side in 1926. The choir and sanctuary were, however, refurnished by a local architect, R. J. Johnson, and his fine new high altar and reredos, choir screen and stalls, and bishop's throne, in a 15th-century style, all survive.

ABOVE RIGHT: This early brass lectern (*c.* 1500) is a very rare survival of pre-Reformation furnishing.

LEFT: The cathedral's great crown steeple was built *c.* 1448, when the cathedral was the parish church of a large and flourishing medieval city. In the foreground stands the mid-13th-century Black Gate into the 'New Castle'.

DEDICATION

- Cathedral Church of St Nicholas

HISTORY

- New castle built to the north of the Tyne in 1080, with the church of St Nicholas just outside it
- The church of St Nicholas was a very large parish church in a major city by *c.* 1500
- New diocese created on 17 May 1882
- Vestry and hall additions in 1926 and 1984

OF SPECIAL INTEREST

- Fourteenth-century crypt chapel (former charnel-house)
- Early 15th-century font and canopy
- Lectern of *c.* 1500
- Flemish brass of Roger Thornton (1441) in south choir aisle
- Renatus Harris organ case (1676)
- New choir and presbytery furnishings, from 1882, by R. J. Johnson

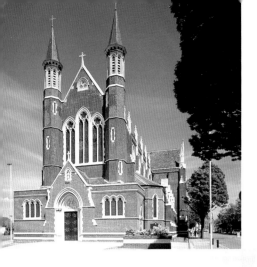

PORTSMOUTH
ROMAN CATHOLIC
HAMPSHIRE

DEDICATION

- Cathedral of St John the Evangelist

HISTORY

- New church, designed by John Crawley, built 1877–82
- West end completed by J. S. Hansom 1886–92
- Narthex, porch, etc., added by A. J. C. Scoles in 1906
- Reordered in 1971 and 2001

OF SPECIAL INTEREST

- New stained glass of 1962 in north transept

ABOVE: The west front of the cathedral was completed in 1906 using the local Fareham red brick.

RIGHT: A fine timber roof and vaults, with a hanging Rood, cover the polygonally ended eastern arm.

his large building suffers today from being right beside the main road from a motorway into the centre of Portsmouth. It also suffered war damage, and sits on an exposed triangular site. A church of St John the Evangelist was first built here from 1877 to 1882, and in 1892 this became the new cathedral for a diocese cut out of the 1850 diocese of Southwark.

The initial design was by John Crawley, but he died in 1880, leaving J. S. Hansom to complete the west end from 1886. Later still, in 1906, a narthex and porch were added to a design by Canon A. J. C. Scoles. The dark-red brick of the exterior is very striking, though it is a pity that the tower and spire on the south-west were not completed. The interior of the building is grand and well-proportioned, with windows in the Decorated style. The large – and very visible – south transept window was perhaps inspired by the great 'bishop's eye' window on the south side of Lincoln Minster. The heart of Portsmouth Cathedral is the crossing, rather than the east end, though sadly the late Victorian Gothic baldacchino, with large marble columns, was taken away in the reordering of 1971.

SOUTHWELL MINSTER

NOTTINGHAMSHIRE

outhwell became a cathedral only in 1884, but long before then it was, along with Ripon and Beverley, one of the three great collegiate minster churches of the archbishops of York in their very large diocese. These churches were, therefore, already 'pro-cathedrals' in the medieval period, and Southwell was the ecclesiastical capital of the southern part of the diocese. Unfortunately, the chapter for this earlier minster was dissolved in 1840 (its property was used to endow Ripon and Manchester cathedrals), and the new cathedral was relatively poor. Ironically, Henry VIII had thought of making it a cathedral, but just after his death the old college was suppressed under the Chantries Act. Ten years later the college was reconstituted, however, and it was this that probably saved the church from ruin.

ABOVE RIGHT: The detail of the carved stone foliage in the chapter house is unsurpassed in England.

BELOW: The early 12th-century western arm of the cathedral has a particularly fine west doorway.

A cathedral of three parts

Though the church was founded in the mid-10th century, the earliest part of the present structure dates from the early 12th century, when Archbishop Thomas II of York started to rebuild completely his Anglo-Saxon collegiate church. The present building is, in fact, made

DEDICATION
- Cathedral and Parish Church of the Blessed Virgin Mary

HISTORY
- Southwell granted to Archbishop Oskytel by King Eadwig *c.* 956
- Present church built by Archbishop Thomas *c.* 1108–50
- Eastern arm greatly enlarged and rebuilt *c.* 1234–50
- Chapter house and vestibule built *c.* 1290–1300
- Pulpitum screen made *c.* 1320
- Chapter dissolved in 1840
- New diocese created for Derbyshire and Nottinghamshire in 1884

OF SPECIAL INTEREST
- Late Anglo-Saxon tympanum in north transept
- The chapter house and vestibule
- The early 12th-century nave and west doorway
- Early 13th-century eastern arm
- Late 13th-century chapter house
- The pulpitum screen
- West window by Patrick Reyntiens
- Ruins of archbishop's palace to south

fine 12th-century north porch – the principal entrance to the church – also survives.

Just before 1233 Archbishop Walter de Gray decided to rebuild the eastern arm of the minster, just as he had done at Beverley and Ripon. For the next 15 years or so, a large new choir and a presbytery were erected for the canons, possibly using masons who had earlier been working at Lincoln Minster. This fine example of Early English work is unusual in having two as its basic unit: there are only two, not three storeys, and the aisle and clerestory windows are in pairs. The east windows, likewise, are of four lights rather then the usual three or five. Unlike the nave, which had a wooden roof, the eastern arm has a beautiful stone-ribbed vault, as well as many fine mouldings in the elevations.

The final glory of Southwell Minster is, however, the superb chapter house of the late 13th century. It is a smaller and later version of the great octagonal chapter houses at Westminster and Salisbury and has no central pillar, though uniquely it does have a stone vault. All round the walls on the capitals is exquisitely carved decoration of naturalistic foliage, and it is easy to spot oak, hawthorn, ivy, vine leaves and other plants, as well as hidden animals.

ABOVE: The early 12th-century nave has a magnificent pulpitum screen of *c.* 1320. The vault beneath this screen has highly unusual flying ribs, similar to those found in Bristol Cathedral.

RIGHT: The beautiful doorway into the octagonal chapter house has wonderful carved decoration and Purbeck marble shafts. Beyond the portal are superb canopied seats, with their exquisite foliage decoration.

up of three principal areas: the earlier 12th-century nave, transepts and towers; the earlier 13th-century eastern arm; and the wonderful late 13th-century chapter house and its entrance passage. The unity of the sturdy Norman western part of the church is only really broken up once by the very large Perpendicular west window. Otherwise it is a fine example of late Romanesque architecture, with round pillars and large semicircular arches – the arches in the triforium being nearly as large as those in the main arcade. There is also a fine pair of contemporary western towers (the timber and lead spires were replaced in 1880), and a very large, relatively low, crossing tower. As well as this, the very

WAKEFIELD
WEST YORKSHIRE

ABOVE RIGHT: The Rood screen designed by Sir Ninian Comper was installed in 1950.

BELOW: The view of the cathedral from the south-east shows Pearson's new east end. Pearson also designed Truro Cathedral.

his is another fine, large, late-medieval parish church that has become a cathedral – in this case in 1888, when the new diocese of Wakefield was created in industrial West Yorkshire. The building that we see today, with its tall tower and spire (247 feet high), is largely a structure of the later 19th and 20th centuries. The reason for this is that, before it became a cathedral, the church had been completely restored by the great Victorian architect, Sir George Gilbert Scott. Scott had found the building in a very poor condition: the whole spire, for example, had to be taken down and rebuilt in 1860, and he also stripped out the old 18th-century pews and galleries.

In 1897, after the death of the first bishop, William Walsham Howe, the architect J. L. Pearson was commissioned to design a new east end with transepts. He died soon afterwards, but his son Frank worked up the sketches and in 1901–5 built the extension, with its fine (if rather mechanically cut) stone lierne vaulting. Having removed the old east wall, Pearson created a new sanctuary just beyond it, with an elaborate new altar and reredos. Perhaps the most notable thing about the late Victorian church is its fine collection of new stained glass, mostly designed by C. E. Kempe (1837–1907) over a period of nearly 40 years.

DEDICATION
• Cathedral Church of All Saints

HISTORY
• Parish church consecrated by Archbishop Melton in 1329
• Church greatly enlarged and tower and spire built in the 15th century
• Spire rebuilt and major restoration 1860–74
• New diocese created in 1888
• New east end built 1901–5

OF SPECIAL INTEREST
• Very tall nave piers (13th- to 14th-century)
• Fifteenth-century carved roof bosses and misericords
• Copy of Anglo-Saxon cross shaft (10th century)
• Much good Kempe stained glass

THE TWENTIETH CENTURY

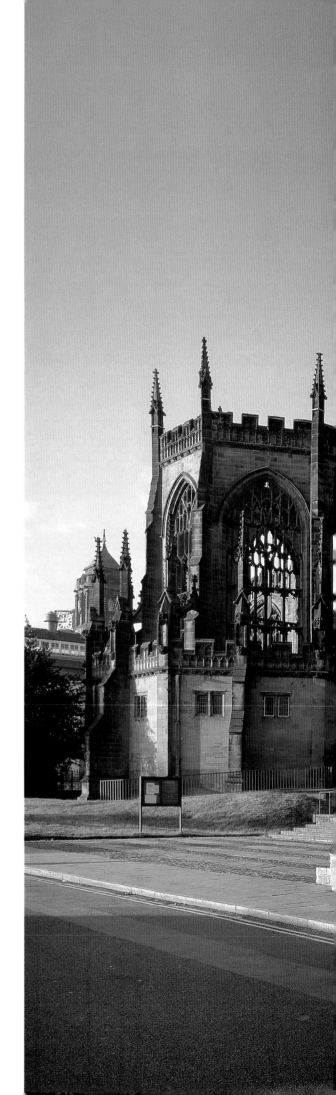

With the preparatory work in the 19th century, the 20th century saw a completely new series of dioceses being made and new cathedrals built. A dozen new dioceses were created between 1905 and 1927, but the building work was hugely hampered by the two World Wars. A bold start was made at Liverpool in 1904, and it is a remarkable achievement that this vast new cathedral was finally finished after 75 years. Elsewhere, however, only Guildford and Coventry were built as completely new cathedrals, and by the time the latter was being finished in the 1960s, a low point in British architecture had been reached. Not only was this the time of concrete and copper, but it was also a time when many fine Victorian furnishings were ruthlessly torn out of both Anglican and Roman Catholic cathedrals. In the last quarter of the century, however, a great deal has been done to conserve sympathetically and repair most of our ancient cathedrals and their uniquely splendid contents. Alongside this, there has been a large increase in the numbers of visitors to the cathedrals. We are also learning much from careful new archaeological and architectural studies of the fabric.

ABOVE: Acclaimed artist Graham Sutherland's tapestry of Christ in Glory adorns Coventry Cathedral.
RIGHT: An exceptionally tall entrance porch connects the new Coventry Cathedral with its burnt-out predecessor. The street side of the cathedral is decorated with Sir Jacob Epstein's statue of *St Michael and the Devil*.

BIRMINGHAM
WEST MIDLANDS

DEDICATION

- Cathedral Church of St Philip

HISTORY

- New parish church established in the rapidly growing 'High Town' area in 1708
- New church built for £5,000 in 1710–15
- Tower and dome added for an extra £600 in 1725
- Chancel enlarged and new stalls put in 1884–8
- New diocese created in 1905
- Cathedral bombed and gutted on 7 November 1940, and restored in 1948
- New undercroft built in 1989

OF SPECIAL INTEREST

- Three eastern and west windows (1885–7 and 1897) made by Sir Edward Burne-Jones (1833–98), a local man
- Organ case of 1715 by Thomas Schwarbrick of Warwick
- Two 18th-century box pews at west end

ABOVE: The dome and cupola of this fine Baroque cathedral are based on the central dome of Santa Maria della Salute in Venice.

t is remarkable that Birmingham, which has grown to be the second largest city in Britain, has such a modest cathedral. If a small city and diocese like Truro could pay for and create a new cathedral, and a large city like Liverpool (though always much smaller than Birmingham) could build a vast new structure, why not Birmingham?

The new diocese was created in 1905, principally by two men: Joseph Chamberlain, a renowned local statesman, and Charles Gore, bishop of Worcester since 1902. Gore was one of the greatest early 20th-century bishops, and he became the first bishop of the new diocese. His pro-cathedral was, however, the fine but quite small church of St Philip, which had been built in the early 18th century by the 'amateur' architect Thomas Archer for the expanding city. Archer had been MP for Warwick in 1660, and had travelled on the Continent for four years looking at the new Baroque architecture; he was much influenced by Bernini and Borromini in Italy, and his style was a good deal more continental than Sir Christopher Wren's.

Birmingham Cathedral is, then, a rectangular Baroque building erected in 1710–15. A fine western tower, capped with a leaded dome and open lantern, was added in 1725. The shallow apsidal chancel was extended in 1884–8 by J. A. Chatwin, making it just big enough for Bishop Gore's new cathedral in 1905. The church had to be refaced in 1864–9, by Chatwin, because the original stone from Thomas Archer's own quarries at Umberslade was too soft (the tower was refaced in 1958–9).

LEFT: In Chatwin's enlarged chancel are three stained-glass windows (1885–7) by Edward Burne-Jones, with the central window representing the Ascension.

SOUTHWARK

LONDON

ABOVE RIGHT: Through the arch on the right of the west wall of the 14th-century south transept a monument to Shakespeare can be glimpsed, while not far from here Shakespeare's plays are performed in the Globe Theatre.

RIGHT: The 13th-century east end was heavily restored in the 19th century after it was found to be unsafe. In the background stands the fine early Perpendicular crossing tower, now the oldest landmark on the South Bank.

his fine building, which stands south-west of London Bridge, became a cathedral only in 1905. It has a long and complicated architectural history that continues to this day: a new 'chapter house' was built outside the north wall of the nave in 1988, and a new refectory, library and shop have just been completed to the east of this.

Early history

Although, there was a late Anglo-Saxon church on this site, the oldest part of the present building – the shell of the north transept – was built in the early 12th century for a new Augustinian priory church called St Mary Overie ('over the river'). This priory had its conventual buildings around a cloister on the north side of the nave, but they were all demolished after the Dissolution. From the middle of the 12th century, the bishops of Winchester had a very large London residence immediately to the west of the church (Southwark was in the north-east corner of the Winchester diocese), and in the later Middle Ages the bishops were great patrons of St Mary Overie. There was a devastating fire at the priory in 1212, but after this Bishop Peter des Roches (1204–38) provided funds for the building of a large new eastern arm which still exists, though it was heavily restored in the 19th century. This eastern arm has both a fine high vaulted presbytery, with early Gothic triforium and clerestory arcades, and a beautiful low-vaulted eastern ambulatory (or retrochoir) with chapels to the east. Unfortunately, the eastern Lady chapel was unnecessarily pulled down in 1830 to make way for the new approach to London Bridge. (Bishop Lancelot Andrewes's tomb was moved from the Lady chapel to the south side of the high altar at this time.) Later in the 13th century the Romanesque north transept was given new Purbeck marble wall-shafts and fine ribbed vaults. The south transept, on the other hand, was completely rebuilt in the 14th century,

DEDICATION

- Cathedral and Collegiate Church of St Saviour and St Mary Overie

HISTORY

- Late Anglo-Saxon church built near south end of London Bridge
- New Augustinian priory of St Mary Overie founded in 1106
- Church burnt in 1212, and new eastern arm built
- Priory dissolved and the church becomes the local parish church in 1539
- Eastern arm restored by Bishop Lancelot Andrewes in 1624
- Tower and eastern arm restored, but nave demolished in the early 19th century
- New nave built 1890–97, and diocese created in 1905

OF SPECIAL INTEREST

- Twelfth-century remains in north transept area
- Thirteenth-century retrochoir and eastern chapels
- Repainted tomb of John Gower, the poet (1408)
- Thirteenth-century choir and presbytery with great screen (c. 1520)
- Tomb of Bishop Lancelot Andrewes made in 1626, and restored in 1930
- Tomb of Edward Talbot (1911), first bishop of Southwark

but it too has been heavily restored. It originally communicated eastwards with the parish church of St Mary Magdalene, but the church was knocked down in 1822. The window tracery and vaulting of the south transept were rebuilt in the late 19th century.

A new diocese

The eastern part of St Mary's was gradually restored in the early part of the 19th century, but the late medieval roof of the nave was removed in 1831, and the rest of the nave was demolished in 1838. Soon afterwards, huge curved railway viaducts, which still survive, were built immediately to the south of the building, much to its detriment. In 1877 Southwark became part of Rochester diocese, but Anthony Thorold, the new bishop of Rochester, set about raising money for a new south London diocese to be based at Southwark. In 1890 a new nave was started, designed by Sir Arthur Blomfield, to fit in with the 13th-century eastern arm. Seven years later St Mary's became a pro-cathedral for south London, and finally in 1905 an Act of Parliament created the new 'Cathedral and Collegiate Church of St Saviour and St Mary Overie'.

LEFT: The great reredos in the sanctuary (restored in 1833) was paid for by Bishop Fox of Winchester in the early 16th century.

BELOW: The tomb of Bishop Lancelot Andrewes (d. 1626) was restored and given a new canopy by Sir Ninian Comper in 1930.

BURY ST EDMUND'S

SUFFOLK

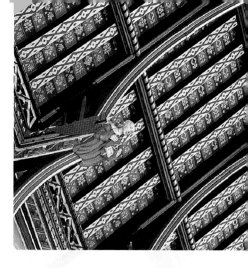

ABOVE RIGHT: Sir George Gilbert Scott's hammer-beam (angel) roof over the nave, which follows a traditional East Anglian form, was painted between 1948 and 1982, adding much-needed colour to the building.

t is a great misfortune that in 1539 the great abbey church at Bury was not turned into a new cathedral, as had been suggested by Henry VIII. Instead, the church was systematically demolished, leaving only the meagre ruins that can now be seen in the fine public gardens.

After old St Paul's and Winchester Cathedral this was the largest great church in England (it was just under 500 feet long), and at the time of the dissolution of the monastery in 1539 it must have been a spectacular church, with its west front alone being nearly 250 feet wide.

Just after the Norman Conquest, the bishop of East Anglia attempted to establish his see in the new town at Bury, but it was not until 1914 that a cathedral church for Suffolk was created within the old abbey precinct and just to the north-west of the abbey church itself.

The present church was first built in the early 16th century to the designs of the royal master mason, John Wastell. The surviving nine-bay nave of the present cathedral is Wastell's work, though its hammer-beam (angel) roof of 1862–4 is by Sir George Gilbert Scott. Scott also rebuilt the chancel, but this was demolished in the 1960s and replaced with a new enlarged eastern arm, designed by Stephen Dykes Bower. New transepts and an aisled choir were built, and this work was completed and consecrated in 1970. To the north of the unfinished north wall of the choir, a new 'cathedral centre' was opened in 1990, and now, at the beginning of a new millennium, work is under way to build a new crossing tower and complete the north transept.

DEDICATION

- Cathedral Church of St James

HISTORY

- Murder of King Edmund in AD 869
- Work starts on huge new Benedictine abbey in 1065
- New church of St James within the abbey precinct started in 1503
- Dissolution and demolition of abbey in 1539
- St James's church enlarged with new chancel in 1711
- Chancel rebuilt and nave restored 1865–9
- Creation of new diocese of St Edmundsbury and Ipswich in 1914
- New porch, cloister walk and eastern arm built 1960–70

OF SPECIAL INTEREST

- Nave arcading (early 16th century)
- Early 18th-century Reynolds monuments at west end of nave
- Nave roof by Sir George Gilbert Scott (1862–4)
- Many mid-20th-century furnishings by Stephen Dykes Bower
- Ruins of Benedictine abbey to the east, and two exceptionally fine abbey gatehouse towers to north and south

RIGHT: The west front of the cathedral at Bury St Edmund's was designed as the Church of St James by royal master mason John Wastell, of King's College Chapel, Cambridge, and Canterbury Cathedral fame. During the cathedral's Victorian restoration by Sir George Gilbert Scott, a more pointed gable was introduced to the west front. In the 1960s, a north-west porch, designed by Stephen Dykes Bower was added (seen here on the left).

CHELMSFORD

ESSEX

ABOVE: Beside Robert Potter's modern altar at the entrance to the chancel is an unusual early 15th-century round arch with open-work panel tracery in the central spandrel.

rom the early 7th century until 1845 Essex was part of the diocese of London. Then, rather oddly, it was joined to west Kent and became part of the diocese of Rochester. In 1877 it was transferred to the newly created St Alban's diocese, until 1913 when a separate diocese was created for Essex, one of the most heavily populated areas in England, with its new *cathedra* in the large parish church of the Virgin in Chelmsford.

This late medieval church has a very fine south porch covered in surface patterns made using knapped flint and dressed stone, otherwise known as flushwork decoration. There is also good flushwork at the top of the tower, which is capped with a tiny lantern of 1749 and a needle spire. The spire was originally covered in lead, but is now sadly copper. In 1800 the nave arcade collapsed when a burial vault was being dug, and it was then completely rebuilt by John Johnson using Coade stone on the south side. Johnson also rebuilt the clerestories and put in a fine coved ceiling. The church was 'restored' in 1873 and an outer north aisle and north transept were built by Sir Arthur Blomfield, who also rebuilt the east window, which still exists, though it has been reset.

No major scheme to enlarge Chelmsford church into a cathedral was conceived, but in 1923–6 Sir Charles Nicholson added two bays to the east end of the chancel, along with a new 'chapter house', muniment room and vestries. A major reordering took place in 1983 when a completely new floor was laid and much colour was added. A new central altar, designed by Robert Potter, was installed, while against the east wall a stone *cathedra* carved by John Skelton was placed.

LEFT: The south porch has very fine late 15th-century flushwork decoration, while the same decoration on the parapets dates from a late 19th-century restoration.

SHEFFIELD
SOUTH YORKSHIRE

he new diocese for the South Yorkshire area was created in 1914, and a parish church, founded in the early 12th century, became the new bishop's seat. Unfortunately, the cathedral church of saints Peter and Paul is today a very muddled complex of buildings, flanked on the south by a modern paved area with Sheffield's new trams running past.

The parish church was in a poor state in the 18th century, and in 1805 the nave and aisles were rebuilt. This was followed by a major restoration in the 1880s, when the transepts were rebuilt and the church was lengthened by 25 feet. After the First World War a scheme was drawn up by Sir Charles Nicholson for a completely new north–south cathedral, retaining only the old east end as a double-aisled transept. The northern part of the new scheme was built in the late 1930s, but this was only the new chapter house, vestries and a chapel of the Holy Spirit. Nicholson died in 1949, and in the 1960s the rest of the scheme was abandoned, and a new nave and 'western crossing' on the old alignment were built instead. This structure, designed by Arthur Bailey, is surmounted by a 'crown of thorns' lantern.

ABOVE RIGHT: The cathedral from the south-west, with the narthex tower over the entrance. 'Narthex' is an early Christian term for a portico or porch outside the west end of a church. Many consider this tower to be a brutal idiosyncrasy and typical of the 1960s.

RIGHT: A 'crown of thorns' lantern surmounts the west end of the nave. Designed by Arthur Bailey, this new nave replaced an original design by Sir Charles Nicholson which was abandoned after Nicholson's death in 1949. Nicholson's unfinished chancel is partly incorporated in St George's Chapel.

DEDICATION

- Cathedral Church of St Peter and St Paul

HISTORY

- Parish church for Sheffield from at least the 12th century
- Nave and aisles rebuilt in 1805
- Transepts rebuilt and east end enlarged in 1880
- Diocese created in 1914
- New cathedral planned and work started in the late 1930s
- New design for west end of nave in 1966

OF SPECIAL INTEREST

- Stalls in Holy Spirit chapel by Sir Ninian Comper
- Tomb of 4th earl of Shrewsbury (*c.* 1538)
- 'Crown of thorns' lantern at west end

BRENTWOOD
ROMAN CATHOLIC
ESSEX

DEDICATION

• Cathedral of St Helen and St Mary

HISTORY

• First church opened in 1837 (still exists to the north of the cathedral)

• New church built 1860–61

• Diocese of Brentwood created in 1917

• Enlargement built to the north 1972–3

• New neo-classical cathedral built 1989–91

OF SPECIAL INTEREST

• New neo-classical interior

• High altar and podium, *cathedra* and *ambo*

• Fine brass chandeliers

ABOVE: The new cathedral has a classical façade.

RIGHT: Old and new: the 1861 and 1989 east walls, side by side.

BELOW: The modern interior, with the old church beyond.

n 1860–61 a rather unattractive church, designed by Gilbert Blount, was erected in the middle of Brentwood, but the first bishop of Brentwood, with his *cathedra* here, was not appointed until 1917.

In the early 1970s the Victorian church started to be transformed with an extension to the north. In 1989, however, work started on adding a spectacular new square building, in the neo-classical style, to the north side of the old church. This splendid structure, designed by Quinlan Terry, is a great success and in two years has completely transformed the old church. The central square space contains the altar, *cathedra* and *ambo* (pulpit), all made in Pisa, Italy, of Nabrasina stone. Beyond, early Italian Renaissance arches open into aisles all around, which contain seating. Above the arcades is a frieze of triglyphs and metopes and a cornice; above this, round-headed clerestory windows bring in light. In the centre of the large flat ceiling is an octagonal opening to the lantern, which sits on the shallow-pitched roof. This lantern, which is similar to the upper part of the lantern at Portsmouth Cathedral, is capped by a small lead dome and a cross. The outer masonry walls also have a frieze of metopes and triglyphs, with a parapet above containing miniature pediments. The remaining part of the old 1861 church survives on the south as the Blessed Sacrament chapel.

COVENTRY
WEST MIDLANDS

oventry Cathedral is now well known as a very modern building, by Sir Basil Spence, which was consecrated in May 1962 after its predecessor, St Michael's, had been burnt out in an air raid in November 1940. This fine parish church had become a cathedral only in 1918, when the new diocese of Coventry was created.

There was already a diocese of Coventry and Lichfield in the Middle Ages, but, tragically, the great medieval monastic cathedral of Coventry was the only English cathedral to be destroyed when Henry VIII dissolved the monasteries. This building was completely pulled down, but we know that it was over 400 feet long because fragments of the west front and of the extreme east end are visible. The foundations of the east end were uncovered in 1955, just outside the west wall of the modern cathedral nave. The huge monastic church had a large semicircular ambulatory around the high altar at its east end. This ambulatory was probably first built soon after the Norman Conquest, before the abbey had become a cathedral. Fragments of the crossing piers, the north transept and the chapter house to the north have very recently been uncovered in an archaeological excavation, and this has allowed the plan to be worked out in more detail. The

ABOVE RIGHT: The view east shows the old burnt-out church, with the porch of the new cathedral behind.

BELOW: Empty traceried windows in the north aisle of the burnt-out shell of the late medieval parish church of St Michael.

foundations of the west end of the nave can now be seen in a garden, where the lowest part of the west wall of the church with two western towers are also visible.

The large Anglo-Saxon diocese for this area was based at Lichfield. However, as at Wells, a monastic church in a Roman walled town was needed for a cathedral, and Chester was chosen. After 20 years (1075–95) this unsatisfactory arrangement was terminated, and the bishop's *cathedra* was moved to the Benedictine abbey at Coventry by Bishop Robert de Lymesey. In the later Middle Ages the diocese was a joint one of Coventry and Lichfield.

In 1837 the Coventry area was removed from Lichfield diocese and joined to Worcester. In 1905 it became part of the new diocese of Birmingham before finally becoming a cathedral city again in 1918, with the fine parish church of St Michael as its cathedral. All that remains of this church are the small northern crypt, the consolidated outer walls and one of the most magnificent towers and spires in England. This had been built in the late 14th century, and was about 300 feet high (it was reduced to the present 295 feet in John Oldrid Scott's restoration of 1889).

Concrete for a modern age

After the destruction of St Michael's in 1940, much discussion about a new cathedral took place, with Sir Giles Gilbert Scott (the architect of Liverpool Cathedral) sketching various schemes. He resigned, however, at the beginning of 1947, and a major competition for a new building was organized. The winner, from 219 entries, was Basil Spence, who produced a radical new design for a concrete and copper-covered cathedral. This was on a north–south axis, with a tall covered porch connecting the new building to the ruins of St Michael's. Work started in 1956 and the new cathedral was consecrated after only six years. The building is clad externally in a local red sandstone, and it contains many modern works of art, perhaps most famously Graham Sutherland's 74-foot-tall tapestry of *Christ in Glory in the Tetramorph*.

LEFT: Graham Sutherland's great tapestry on the north wall was woven in one piece in France using Australian wool. It is the largest tapestry in the world, and dominates the sanctuary and choir.

BRADFORD

WEST YORKSHIRE

ABOVE RIGHT: The peaceful cathedral close, on the cathedral's north-west side, contains the houses of the deans and canons.

erched on a hillside on the east of the city, the parish church of St Peter became the cathedral for north-west Yorkshire, as well as small parts of Cumbria and Lancashire, in 1919. It was originally a fine, large, aisled parish church of the late Middle Ages, and to this was added a 100-foot-high west tower at the beginning of the 16th century. All of this shows that it had become a prosperous 'wool' church and, along with Wakefield and Halifax, one of the three great town churches of the West Riding of Yorkshire.

During the later 19th century the whole church was heavily restored, and the east end was demolished and rebuilt with new north and south transepts. The fine William Morris glass in the present east windows is all that now survives of the seven-light 1863 east window.

After the Second World War plans were finally put in hand to make Bradford look more like a cathedral, and a first stage of this work was the building of two new wings to the north and south of the west tower in the 1950s. Then a completely new eastern arm, designed by Sir Edward Maufe, the architect of the new Guildford Cathedral, was built in the early 1960s; this new work can clearly be seen as one moves eastwards down the old nave. The external cleaning of the whole building has done much to unify the structure, which is now set in a small close – where the dean and two canons have their houses – with fine gardens on the hillside to the south and west of the cathedral.

LEFT: Behind the high altar in Sir Edward Maufe's new eastern arm lies the Lady chapel, with stained glass by William Morris in its east window.

DEDICATION

• Cathedral Church of St Peter

HISTORY

• Large parish church by 15th century, with new west tower added in 1508

• Transepts and new east end added in 1863 and 1898 respectively

• New diocese created in 1919

• Wings added to west tower (for offices and song room) in 1956

• New east end built 1963–5

OF SPECIAL INTEREST

• Fragment of late Anglo-Saxon cross shaft in north choir aisle

• Font and cover (15th century)

• Memorial, by Flaxman, to Abraham Balme (1796)

• East window by William Morris & Co. (1863)

LANCASTER

ROMAN CATHOLIC

LANCASHIRE

DEDICATION

• Cathedral Church of St Peter

HISTORY

• Church of St Peter built 1853–9

• Octagonal baptistery added to the north transept in 1901

• Diocese of Lancaster created in 1924

• Reordering and restoration of old sanctuary in 1995

OF SPECIAL INTEREST

• Statue of St Peter (replica of statue in St Peter's, Rome)

• Fittings in Blessed Sacrament chapel (original sanctuary), designed by Sir Giles Gilbert Scott (1909)

• The baptistery

• Some good Victorian stained glass

ABOVE: The cathedral's impressive spire was designed by local architect Edward Paley.

hough the diocese of Lancaster, which covers Cumbria and northern Lancashire, was created only in 1924, the fine cathedral with its 240-foot-high spire was built as St Peter's Church in 1853–9. This was after Father Richard Brown had acquired a three-acre plot on the edge of Lancaster in 1847 for a cemetery, school and convent. Brown commissioned local architect Edward Graham Paley to design a completely new church in the Decorated Gothic (early 14th-century) style, and it is this large church that suitably became a cathedral in 1924.

There is a large aisled nave, north and south transepts, and a chancel ending in a polygonal east end. East of the north transept is the Lady chapel, with a veined marble altar and reredos. The smaller St Charles Borromeo chapel runs east from the south transept, with the elaborate Sacred Heart marble altar beside it. The church also contains, on the south side, two small chantry chapels – one for the Whitesides and one for the Coulstons – and a lot of good 19th-century glass. An octagonal baptistery was added to the north transept in 1901. In 1995 the cathedral was reordered, and at the same time the old sanctuary to the east was restored to its original earlier state, and is now the Blessed Sacrament chapel. Notable among the contents is Sir Giles Gilbert Scott's large triptych of 1909.

RIGHT: The reordered crossing area has a new altar and bishop's throne (the cathedral's old throne can be seen in the north transept). Behind the altar is the restored Blessed Sacrament chapel.

BLACKBURN

LANCASHIRE

ABOVE RIGHT: The lantern and flèche above the east end of the cathedral add a distinctively 1960s' touch to the building.

he parish church of St Mary the Virgin in Blackburn became a cathedral in 1926 when a new diocese was needed for Lancashire, separate from the hugely populous diocese of Manchester. Within a few years the cathedral architect and surveyor, W. A. Forsyth, had produced designs for a much larger church, which retained only the aisled nave and west tower of the earlier parish church. This church had been built in 1820–26 by John Palmer, and was an early example of the Gothic revival in the Decorated style.

The foundation stone for Forsyth's new eastern arm was laid in 1938, at exactly the same time as he was supervising the restoration of the tower and spire of Salisbury Cathedral. The year 1938 was not a good one to start major building works, though, and the war soon put a stop to the work. It was started again in 1950, and construction continued slowly on the new transepts, crossing and east end.

In 1961 a new architect, Laurence King, took over, and Forsyth's planned octagonal tower with a lantern on top was dropped. Instead, King built a low modern octagonal lantern with a corona-like top. Capping this is a tall and very thin spire (or flèche). The work was finally finished in 1967, but the new corona and flèche sadly do not, in any way, tie in with the earlier Gothic revival west tower.

RIGHT: View west down the nave with the *Christ the Worker* sculpture by John Hayward on the west wall.

DEDICATION

- Cathedral Church of St Mary the Virgin with St Paul

HISTORY

- Medieval parish church rebuilt 1820–26
- New diocese created in 1926
- Work on new eastern arm, 1938–9, with a break until 1950
- Scheme modified due to lack of money in 1961
- New lantern and flèche completed in 1967

OF SPECIAL INTEREST

- Medieval stalls (and misericords) and 'original' bishop's throne in north transept
- North transept five-light window (former east window of parish church)
- Many good modern furnishings
- New fibre-optic sculpture, *The Healing of the Nations* by Mark Jalland (2001), on the exterior of the cathedral's east end

DERBY
DERBYSHIRE

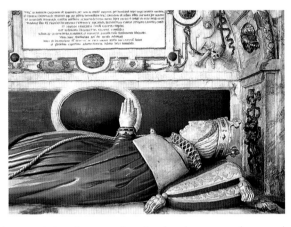

DEDICATION

• Cathedral Church of All Saints

HISTORY

• Large late medieval parish church, with west tower added *c.* 1520

• New early Georgian church built in 1723–5

• Visit of 'Bonnie Prince Charlie' to the cathedral on 4–6 December 1745

• Diocese of Derby created on 28 October 1927

• New eastern extension built 1965–72

OF SPECIAL INTEREST

• Tomb of Bess of Hardwick

• Choir screen by Robert Bakewell (1730)

• New classical font of Pentelic marble (1974)

• Bishop's throne, made from 17th-century seat from Constantinople

• Stainless steel portable font made by local apprentices at Rolls-Royce (1987)

ABOVE: Sebastian Comper's new east end was built between 1965 and 1972.

RIGHT: The effigy of Bess of Hardwick, or Elizabeth, countess of Shrewsbury (d. 1607), lies in the south choir aisle.

erby Cathedral is a fine, large parish church which became a cathedral only in 1927 when a new diocese for the county of Derbyshire was formed out of the neighbouring ones of Lichfield and Southwell. Unlike so many other cathedrals the building can be explained very simply, both on a plan and volumetrically. On the west there is a fine, tall Perpendicular tower, which measures 212 feet high and was built *c.* 1520. Next to this is a 'new' parish church of the early 18th century with an aisled nave and chancel all within a rectangular box. Finally, on the east there is the very new, but in keeping, chancel, or retrochoir. This was built on a basement, as the hillside falls away to the east, between 1965 and 1972 in order to make the church look more like a cathedral.

Before the Reformation there was a large, rich collegiate church here. The fine tower with its ring of 10 bells, is all that survives of this church thanks to the vicar, the eccentric Dr Michael Hutchinson who, early one morning in February 1723, rapidly started to demolish the church as a protest at the dilatory local corporation.

A completely new church was then built to the designs of James Gibbs (best known as the architect of St Martin-in-the-Fields, London). This church survived intact until 1965, when the new eastern extension was added by Sebastian Comper, son of the well-known Sir Ninian Comper, who had already provided a more grandiose, but unbuilt, design for the east end.

LEFT: Robert Bakewell's magnificent screen of 1730 decorates the nave. In the distance is the monument to Bess of Hardwick.

LEICESTER
LEICESTERSHIRE

ABOVE RIGHT: The east end of the nave is seen through 14th-century arcading.

I n the late 7th century the Anglo-Saxon bishop for Mercia had his seat in a church in the old Roman city of Ratae Coritanorum (Leicester), and a new cathedral seems to have been built here in 737. This was destroyed by the Vikings in the 9th century, and its site is not known. In the later Anglo-Saxon period the see was absorbed into the vast diocese of Dorchester (later Lincoln), which stretched from the Thames to the Humber.

In 1143 a large new abbey church was built for the Augustinian canons just to the north of the city, and the infamous Cardinal Wolsey died and was buried there in 1530. This church would have made a fine cathedral, but unfortunately it was destroyed after the Dissolution.

When a new diocese for Leicestershire was created in 1927, the civic parish church of St Martin's, in the very centre of Leicester, was chosen as the new cathedral. This church has several fragments of 13th to 16th-century architecture in it, but most of it dates from large scale rebuilding and restoration work in the 19th century. The Norman crossing tower was deemed unsafe and taken down in 1861, and replaced by a tall central tower and stone broach spire (220 feet tall). The eastern arm was also completely rebuilt, while in 1897 a new Perpendicular-style south-west porch was built as the main entrance by J. L. Pearson.

RIGHT: The east window, with glass by Christopher Whall commemorating Leicester men killed in the First World War, framed by the choir screen.

DEDICATION

- Cathedral Church of St Martin

HISTORY

- Civic parish church in the town from at least the 12th century
- Church heavily restored, and chancel and tower and spire rebuilt 1844–67
- South porch built in 1897
- Diocese created in 1927

OF SPECIAL INTEREST

- Furnishings of 18th-century archdeacon's consistory court (now used for bishop's consistory court)
- Inscriptions in choir floor commemorating Richard III, who died nearby at the Battle of Bosworth, 1485
- Large Snetzler organ in west gallery (1774)

PORTSMOUTH
HAMPSHIRE

ABOVE: Michael Drury's 1990 west front.

RIGHT: The chancel has late 12th-century arcades, while beyond the high altar are tall columns of the late 17th-century church.

BELOW: The nave's west end was designed by Sir Charles Nicholson in 1935 but finished by Michael Drury in 1991.

ike Guildford, the diocese of Portsmouth was cut out of the large Winchester diocese in 1927. Unlike Guildford, however, the fine church of St Thomas of Canterbury in the historic centre of Portsmouth became the pro-cathedral, and was then enlarged.

The original chapel of St Thomas was built by the Augustinian canons of nearby Southwick Priory in the 1180s. The east end of the present church (aisled chancel and transepts) probably dates from soon after this, when Portsmouth was first becoming an important naval base for King Richard I. Despite major restoration work in 1843, when a high (plaster) vault was reinstalled, there are still some fine architectural features dating from *c.* 1200. The chapel became a parish church in the early 14th century, but unfortunately the west tower was demolished in 1642, when the royalists were using it as a lookout tower during the English Civil War. In 1683 Charles II agreed a brief for its rebuilding, and £9,000 was raised to make a new nave and west tower, which were built in 1691–3 – at the same time as Wren's great new cathedral in London. The octagonal belfry, dome and lantern on top of the tower date from this time.

Five years after the church became a cathedral, Sir Charles Nicholson produced his first sketch plan for the new cathedral (at a chapter meeting in 1932), and from 1935–9 the building was greatly enlarged on the west with a new aisled nave in a 'German' Romanesque style. Low outer ambulatories were also built alongside the old and new naves, and the tower was pierced for a new organ gallery. After the Second World War the work did not recommence. Only in 1990–91 was the west end, which fits in well with the original Nicholson scheme, completed by architect Michael Drury.

GUILDFORD

SURREY

ABOVE RIGHT: Guildford Cathedral, with its south porch arcade and the tower, which is crowned by a golden angel that turns and glints in the wind.

part from Liverpool, this is the only Anglican cathedral to have been built on a completely new site in the 20th century. The great medieval diocese of Winchester, which stretched from the Isle of Wight to London, now has Southwark in its north-east section. In 1927 two further dioceses were cut out of it, based in Portsmouth and Guildford. The pro-cathedral in the church of the Holy Trinity in Guildford could not be enlarged, so a fine new site was found on top of Stag Hill in the old royal park to the north-west of the town. An open competition was held in 1932, and a design by Sir Edward Maufe was chosen. Work on the east end went ahead straight away, but because of the war it was halted between 1939 and 1952. The chancel and crossing were opened in 1954 and the nave was complete by 1961, with small western porches completed by 1964.

The building itself is constructed entirely of brick in a plain, 20th-century Gothic style, with a Doulting stone facing on the inside. The interior is certainly much more successful than the exterior: on entering the cathedral through the western narthex, there is a fine, large open space right through the nave and chancel to the plain east wall of the sanctuary. Behind the high altar is a very large, 45-foot-high curtain with a small round window above. The aisles are remarkably tall and narrow, and the whole building seems to reflect the austerity of the immediate post-war era. The most striking external feature is the tall crossing tower, capped by a golden angel.

LEFT: The positive organ is located in a gallery above the sub-dean's stall and the northern choir stalls. The minimalism of the interior, with its polished Purbeck stone paving, is striking.

DEDICATION

- Cathedral Church of the Holy Spirit

HISTORY

- Diocese created with *cathedra* in Holy Trinity church, Guildford, in 1927
- New eastern arm built on Stag Hill 1936–9
- Work continued and nave built 1952–61
- Consecration of cathedral on 17 May 1961
- Western arcades and porches completed in 1964

OF SPECIAL INTEREST

- Many colourful embroidered kneelers in nave
- Various mid-20th-century furnishings

ARUNDEL
ROMAN CATHOLIC
WEST SUSSEX

DEDICATION

- Cathedral of Our Lady and St Philip Howard

HISTORY

- Built by J. A. Hansom 1870–73
- Diocese of Arundel and Brighton created in 1965
- Shrine made in north transept for St Philip Howard in 1971

OF SPECIAL INTEREST

- West doorway, and statues and rose window above
- Much good stone carving, including stone carvings in the apse, by Farmer & Brindley (1870–73)
- Good late Victorian stained glass, designed by Hansom and made by John Hardman Powell
- Shrine in north transept (1971)

ABOVE: The cathedral stands high above the city's rooftops and is particularly impressive at night.

RIGHT: J. A. Hansom's apsidal chancel has heavy buttresses and pinnacles to support the stone-ribbed vaults inside.

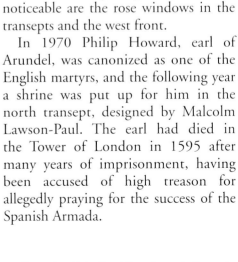

his remarkable late Victorian church, in the French Gothic style, became a cathedral only in 1965, when the new diocese of Arundel and Brighton was created. It was built from 1870 to 1873 for the 15th duke of Norfolk, whose great castle stands nearby. In fact the castle and the church now dominate the town of Arundel, making it look more French than English. The duke's architect was a remarkable man called Joseph Aloysius Hansom, who also produced the large spires for Newcastle and Plymouth cathedrals. He was perhaps best known, however, for designing Birmingham town hall and inventing the 'Hansom cab'.

Arundel Cathedral has a very tall nave, transepts and apsed chancel, and is rib-vaulted throughout. Sadly the eastern Lady chapel and the great north-western tower and spire (meant to be 280 feet high) were never built. Inside the building is a magnificent series of eight-shafted piers, which divide the narrow aisles and the ambulatory. There are many fine windows in the aisles and at clerestory level, filled with good glass; particularly noticeable are the rose windows in the transepts and the west front.

In 1970 Philip Howard, earl of Arundel, was canonized as one of the English martyrs, and the following year a shrine was put up for him in the north transept, designed by Malcolm Lawson-Paul. The earl had died in the Tower of London in 1595 after many years of imprisonment, having been accused of high treason for allegedly praying for the success of the Spanish Armada.

LEFT: The modern high altar at the entrance to Hansom's splendid apsidal sanctuary.

NORWICH

ROMAN CATHOLIC

NORFOLK

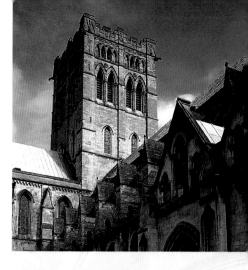

ABOVE RIGHT: The tall crossing tower is a striking feature of the Norwich skyline.

BELOW LEFT: The elaborate iron-covered west door is set into a doorway with Frosterley marble shafting.

BELOW RIGHT: The large Rood and Rood-beam dominate the nave and the chancel.

he new diocese for East Anglia was created only in 1976, but this magnificent church was built between 1884 and 1910 for the 15th duke of Norfolk, who also paid for Arundel Cathedral. Norwich is now by far England's finest Victorian Roman Catholic cathedral. It sits on a very prominent site just to the west of the medieval walled city, where the old city gaol had been. The initial designer was George Gilbert Scott junior, but when he died in 1897 his younger brother, John Oldrid Scott, continued the work to completion in 1910. The nave was built first, so this is entirely by G. G. Scott junior, but the more elaborate chancel is by both brothers. The north transept, particularly the lancet windows, we are told, was in part designed by the patron, the duke of Norfolk.

This magnificent church is 275 feet in length, with a long aisled nave and shorter aisled chancel. There are also substantial transepts, and stone vaults are used throughout the building, with prominent flying buttresses outside. The main style is Early English, with only lancet windows being used, and inside there is much finely carved work and shafting of polished black Frosterley marble. The windows are also filled with very good stained glass, though some of this was destroyed in the Second World War and subsequently replaced. Drawing the whole building together is a tall crossing tower with a crenellated parapet; it is slightly odd that this is not capped by a spire.

DEDICATION

- Cathedral Church of St John the Baptist

HISTORY

- Nave of the church of St John built 1884–1894
- Chancel and transepts finally completed in 1910
- Diocese of East Anglia created in 1976

OF SPECIAL INTEREST

- Much good early 20th-century stained glass by John and Dunstan Powell
- Good carved capitals by James Ovens
- New pulpit by Anthony Rossi (1961)

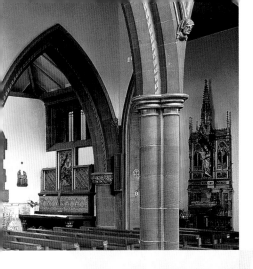

SHEFFIELD (HALLAM)

ROMAN CATHOLIC

SOUTH YORKSHIRE

DEDICATION

- Cathedral Church of St Marie

HISTORY

- Church of St Marie built 1847–50
- 'Munster' Lady chapel added 1878–9
- Reordering of church in 1971
- Creation of diocese of Hallam in 1980

OF SPECIAL INTEREST

- Monument (and effigy) for Father Pratt, under the altar in the 'Mortuary chapel', to the north of the north aisle
- Much fine Victorian stained glass and other furnishings (though much was removed in 1971)

ABOVE: This view from the nave takes in the north aisle and the east end of the 'Mortuary chapel'.

RIGHT: Beyond the north aisle lies the Blessed Sacrament chapel, while to the aisle's left is the 'Mortuary chapel' with Father Pratt's monument beneath the altar.

he new diocese of Hallam, for the south Yorkshire area, was created only in 1980, having been cut out of Leeds. The fine church, which is now the second Sheffield Cathedral, was earlier St Marie's Roman Catholic church, built between 1847 (the foundation stone was laid on 25 March) and 1850. Sadly the priest who had done so much to get it built, Father Charles Pratt, died – aged only 38 – a year before it was completed. His effigy, holding a model of the church, has been mutilated and now lies under an altar in the 'Mortuary chapel'.

The cathedral's architect was Matthew Hadfield, who also designed Salford Cathedral; Hadfield was a friend of A. W. N. Pugin, the designer of many new Roman Catholic cathedrals after the Emancipation Act. The style of the building is early 14th-century Gothic, and Heckington church in Lincolnshire is partly the model. The most obvious feature of the church is the tall south-west tower and spire, just under 200 feet high. Inside the building there were many fine furnishings of the later 19th century, which, as in all Roman Catholic churches, were disturbed and, in part, removed after the reordering demanded by the Second Vatican Council. Much can still be seen, however, and the Hardman glass of the west window, designed by Pugin, is particularly good. Pugin also designed the reredos in 1850 (it was carved by Theodore Phyffers). In 1878–9 a Lady chapel was added, also by Hadfield, and this also contains good Hardman glass.

GLOSSARY

ABBEY Independent monastery with an abbot as its head

AMBULATORY Processional walk round the eastern arm of a large church, especially the aisle enclosing an apse

AMBO Raised reading desk found in early churches; similar to a pulpit

APSE Semicircular recess, usually on the east, for an altar

ARCADE Series of arches

BALDACCHINO Large canopy over an altar, usually supported by columns

BAY Section of wall between external buttresses and internal piers

BENEDICTINE The most important, and earliest, order of monks (or nuns) who follow the Rule of St Benedict

BOSS Large, usually carved, knob at the intersection of vault ribs

CANON Priest in a secular (non-monastic) cathedral, who had his own stall and income from a prebend (a member of 'chapter'), as well as his own house in the Close

CANONIZATION Process of declaring someone a saint by the Pope. From the early 13th century this became a much more bureaucratic affair

CAPITAL The top, often decorated, section of a column

CATHEDRA Bishop's ceremonial chair or throne. Originally placed on the axis of a cathedral (for example at Norwich Cathedral or Canterbury Cathedral), but later *cathedrae* became more elaborate and they are now placed on the south side of the presbytery

CHANTRY CHAPEL Special chapel created for an important person or family in which a priest said masses for the deceased. Abolished by law during the Reformation of 1548

CHAPTER Body of canons with stalls in the choir, and a seat in the chapter house

CHAPTER HOUSE Meeting place for monks or canons; usually a separate rectangular or octagonal building

CHEVRON V-shaped carved decoration, common on 12th-century arches or piers

CHOIR Area of stalls in a cathedral from which services are said or sung

CIBORIUM A canopied shrine for the reserved sacrament or a cover for an altar; similar to a baldacchino

CLERESTORY Windowed upper part of a wall, above the aisle roofs

CLOISTERS Square or rectangle of covered walks beside a cathedral. In a monastery they connected the church with the chapter house, dormitory, refectory, etc.

CLOSE Usually walled precinct around a secular cathedral containing the canons' houses, as well as the cathedral, cemetery, etc.

CORBEL Large projecting block, usually of stone and often carved

COSMATI Name given to 12th- and 13th-century Italian decorative work using inlaid porphyry, marble, etc. Revived in England in the later 19th century

CROSSING Area, often under a tower, between the north and south transepts. Sometimes the choir is here (for example at Winchester Cathedral)

CRYPT Space below a cathedral, usually in the eastern arm

DEAN Senior canon in a secular cathedral, whose stall was on the south side of the western entrance to the choir

DECORATED English architectural style from *c.* 1290 to *c.* 1350, taking its name from the type of tracery used at this time

EARLY ENGLISH English architectural style from *c.* 1175 to *c.* 1245, when the pointed arch (and the Gothic style) made its first appearance

EASTER SEPULCHRE Tomb-like recess on the north side of the sanctuary, holding the Reserved Sacrament between Maundy Thursday and Easter Sunday

FAN VAULT Vault of concave semi-cones without ribs

GEOMETRIC English architectural style from *c.* 1245 to *c.* 1290, taking its name from the form of tracery used at this time

GOTHIC Name given to medieval architecture between *c.* 1175 and *c.* 1540 – sub-phases are Early English, Geometric, Decorated and Perpendicular

LADY CHAPEL Chapel in honour of the Blessed Virgin Mary and, from the 13th century, usually the most important chapel in the cathedral. From the 15th century, Lady chapels had their own choir of professional singers (with boys) to sing polyphonic Lady Masses

LANCET Tall late 12th- to 13th-century window with a pointed head

LIERNE VAULT Vault with small extra ribs in the upper part

MISERICORD Carved bracket on the lower side of a hinged stall seat to support a standing occupant of the stall

NAVE The body or western part of a cathedral, often very long, and usually with aisles. It sometimes has the choir at its east end (for example Westminster Abbey)

NEW FOUNDATION Dean and chapter of a former monastic cathedral, usually created by Henry VIII in 1541

PARAPET Low wall on top of a large wall at the base of a roof

PERPENDICULAR English architectural style from *c.* 1340 to *c.* 1540

PIER Supporting pillar in an arcade

PISCINA Shallow basin with a drain for washing vessels used during Mass, usually in a wall to the south of an altar

PREBEND Part of the cathedral's revenue given to a canon as his stipend (often income from a church or manor), hence from the 16th century a canon was often called a prebendary

PRECENTOR Second most important canon at a secular cathedral, whose stall was on the north side of the western entrance to the choir. A minor canon in a New Foundation

PRESBYTERY Area of a cathedral, east of the choir, containing the sanctuary (high altar, etc.)

PRIORY Cathedral monastery with a bishop as its titular head, but under the control of a prior

PULPITUM SCREEN Large stone screen on the west side of the choir (hence also choir screen), on top of which the organ was often placed

REREDOS Screen or wall-decoration behind and above an altar

RETROCHOIR Area outside the choir, sometimes the name given to the area behind the high altar where a shrine was situated

ROMANESQUE Architectural style in western Europe of the 11th and 12th centuries, when the round arch was used; often called 'Norman' in England

ROOD The crucifixion, flanked by St Mary and St John, usually on top of a beam or Rood screen at the eastern end of the nave. Destroyed by law in 1548, but are often found in 19th-century (especially Roman Catholic) cathedrals

SANCTUARY East end of the presbytery with the high altar at the centre, behind which was sometimes a large screen. To the north was often the Easter Sepulchre, and to the south the sedilia

SECULAR CATHEDRAL Cathedral run by canons and vicars led by a dean, and from Henry VIII's time called an 'Old Foundation'

SEDILIA Usually three canopied seats, for priests, on the south side of the sanctuary

TESTER Flat wooden board or canopy over a pulpit, tomb or shrine

TIERCERON VAULT Vault with three extra ribs springing from the corners of the bays

TRACERY Intersecting ribs on vaults, blank arches, or in the upper part of a window

TRANSEPTS North and south projections, usually from the crossing, in a cathedral. They sometimes have aisles

TRIFORIUM Gallery, usually above the aisles and with a lean-to roof

VAULT Arched ceiling, usually with ribs of stone or timber

VICAR Canon's deputy, with a lower stall in the choir

VICARS' CLOSE Separate area (often walled) within the cathedral close made for the vicars' houses in the late Middle Ages

ADDRESSES & DIOCESAN MAP

ARUNDEL RC CATHEDRAL Cathedral House, Parsons Hill, Arundel, West Sussex BN18 9AY Tel: 01903 882297 www.dabnet.org/arundel.htm

BATH ABBEY The Abbey Office, 13 Kingston Buildings, Bath BA1 1LT Tel: 01225 422462/446300 www.bathabbey.org

BIRMINGHAM CATHEDRAL Colmore Row, Birmingham B3 2QB Tel 0121 236 4333

BIRMINGHAM RC CATHEDRAL Cathedral House, St Chad's Queensway, Birmingham B4 6EU Tel: 0121 236 2251

BLACKBURN CATHEDRAL Cathedral Office, Cathedral Close, Blackburn BB1 5AA Tel: 01254 51491 www.blackburn.anglican.org/cathedral/

BRADFORD CATHEDRAL (Cathedral Church of St Peter) 1 Barkerend Road, Bradford BD3 9AF Tel: 01274 777734 www.bradford.anglican.org/cathedral/

BRENTWOOD RC CATHEDRAL Clergy House, Ingrave Road, Brentwood, Essex CM15 8AT Tel: 01277 210107 www.brentwood-cathedral.co.uk

BRISTOL CATHEDRAL College Green, Bristol BS1 5TJ Tel: 0117 9264879 www.bristol-cathedral.co.uk

BURY ST EDMUNDS CATHEDRAL Cathedral Office, Abbey House, Angel Hill, Bury St Edmunds, Suffolk IP33 1LS Tel: 01284 754 933 www.stedscathedral.co.uk

CANTERBURY CATHEDRAL Cathedral House, 11 The Precincts, Canterbury CT1 2EH Tel: 01227 762862 www.canterbury-cathedral.org

CARLISLE CATHEDRAL Cathedral Office, 7 The Abbey, Carlisle, Cumbria CA3 8TZ Tel: 01228 548151 www.carlislecathedral.org.uk

CHELMSFORD CATHEDRAL Cathedral Office, New Street, Chelmsford, Essex CM1 1TY Tel: 01245 294480 www.cathedral.chelmsford.anglican.org

CHESTER CATHEDRAL 12 Abbey Square, Chester CH1 2HU Tel: 01244 324756 www.chestercathedral.org.uk

CHICHESTER CATHEDRAL The Visitors' Office, The Royal Chantry, Cathedral Cloisters, Chichester, West Sussex P019 1PX Tel: 01243 782595 www.fransnet.clara.net/chicath

CLIFTON RC CATHEDRAL Clifton Cathedral House, Clifton Park, Bristol BS8 3BX Tel: 0117 973 8411 www.cliftoncathedral.org.uk

COVENTRY CATHEDRAL 7 Priory Row, Coventry CV1 5ES Tel: 0247 622 7597 www.coventrycathedral.org

DERBY CATHEDRAL Cathedral Office, 1A College Place, Derby DE1 3DY Tel: 01332 341201 www.derbycathedral.org

DURHAM CATHEDRAL The Chapter Office, The College, Durham DH1 3EH Tel: 0191 386 4266 www.durhamcathedral.co.uk

ELY CATHEDRAL Chapter House, The College, Ely, Cambridgeshire CB7 4DL Tel: 01353 667735 www.cathedral.ely.anglican.org

EXETER CATHEDRAL 1 The Cloisters, Exeter EX1 1HS Tel: 01392 214219 www.exeter-cathedral.org.uk

GLOUCESTER CATHEDRAL The Chapter Office, 2 College Green, Gloucester GL1 2LR Tel: 01452 528095 www.gloucestercathedral.uk.com

GUILDFORD CATHEDRAL Stag Hill, Guildford GU2 7UP Tel: 01483 565287 www.guildford-cathedral.org.uk

HEREFORD CATHEDRAL The Visits Office, 5 College Cloisters, Cathedral Close, Hereford HR1 2NG Tel: 01432 374202 www.aph.org.uk/whattosee/page64.htm

LANCASTER RC CATHEDRAL Cathedral House, Balmoral Road, Lancaster LA1 3BT Tel: 01524 61860 www.lancastercathedral.org.uk

LEEDS RC CATHEDRAL Cathedral House, Great George Street, Leeds LS2 8BE Tel: 0113 245 3626 www.leedsdiocese.org.uk/cathedral/cathedral.html

LEICESTER CATHEDRAL The Cathedral Centre, 21 St Martin's, Leicester LE1 5DE Tel: 0116 262 5294 www.cathedral.leicester.anglican.org

LICHFIELD CATHEDRAL 19A The Close, Lichfield, Staffordshire WS13 7LD Tel: 01543 306100 www.lichfield-cathedral.org

LINCOLN MINSTER Communications Office, Lincoln LN2 1PX Tel: 01522 544544 www.lincolncathedral.com

LIVERPOOL CATHEDRAL St James Mount, Liverpool L1 7AZ Tel: 0151 709 6271 Email: helen.wilson@liverpoolcathedral.org.uk

LIVERPOOL RC CATHEDRAL Cathedral House, Mount Pleasant, Liverpool L3 5TQ Tel: 0151 709 9222 www.liverpool-rc-cathedral.org.uk

MANCHESTER CATHEDRAL Manchester M3 1SX Tel: 0161 833 2220 www.dws.ndirect.co.uk/mc1.htm

MIDDLESBROUGH RC CATHEDRAL Dalby Way, Coulby Newham, Middlesbrough TS8 0RJ Tel: 01642 597750 www.middlesbrough-diocese.org.uk/mass.mid.htm

NEWCASTLE UPON TYNE CATHEDRAL Newcastle upon Tyne NE1 1PF Tel: 0191 232 1939 Email: stnicholas@aol.com

NEWCASTLE UPON TYNE RC CATHEDRAL Clayton Street West, Newcastle upon Tyne NE1 5HH Tel: 0191 232 6953 www.stmaryscathedral.org.uk

NORTHAMPTON RC CATHEDRAL Cathedral House, Kingsthorpe Road, Northampton NN2 6AG Tel: 01604 714556 www.northamptondiocese.org/pages/bishop/bishopframe.htm

NOTTINGHAM RC CATHEDRAL Cathedral House, North Circus Street, Nottingham NG1 5AE Tel: 0115 953 9839 Email: stbarnabas@rccathedral.freeserve.co.uk

NORWICH CATHEDRAL 12 The Close, Norwich NR1 4DH Tel: 01603 218300 www.cathedral.org.uk

NORWICH RC CATHEDRAL Cathedral House, Unthank Road, Norwich, Norfolk NR2 2PA Tel: 01603 624615 www.stjohncathedral.co.uk

OXFORD CATHEDRAL Oxford OX1 1DP Tel: 01865 276155 www.chch.ox.ac.uk

PETERBOROUGH CATHEDRAL Little Prior's Gate, Minster Precincts, Peterborough PE1 1XS Tel: 01733 560964 www.peterborough-cathedral.org.uk

PLYMOUTH RC CATHEDRAL The Cathedral House, Cecil Street, Plymouth PL1 5HW Tel: 01752 662537 www.plymouthcathedral.co.uk

PORTSMOUTH CATHEDRAL Cathedral Office, St Thomas's Street, Old Portsmouth, Hampshire PO1 2HH Tel: 023 9282 3300 www.portsmouthcathedral.org.uk

PORTSMOUTH RC CATHEDRAL Edinburgh Road, Portsmouth, Hants PO1 3HG Tel: 023 9282 6170 www.portsmouth-dio.org.uk/Cathedral/

RIPON MINSTER Ripon Cathedral Office, Liberty Court House, Minster Road, Ripon, North Yorkshire HG4 1QS Tel: 01765 602072 www.riponcathedral.org.uk

ROCHESTER CATHEDRAL Cathedral Office, Garth House, The Precinct, Kent NE1 1SX Tel: 01634 843366 www.rochester.anglican.org/cathedral/

ST ALBAN'S CATHEDRAL St Albans, Hertfordshire AL1 1BY Tel: 01727 860780 www.stalbanscathedral.org.uk

ST PAUL'S CATHEDRAL London EC4M 8AD Tel: 020 7236 4128 www.stpauls.co.uk

SALFORD RC CATHEDRAL Cathedral House, 250 Chapel Street, Salford M3 5LL Tel: 0161 834 0333 www.wardleyhall.org.uk

SALISBURY CATHEDRAL 33 The Close, Salisbury, Wiltshire SP1 2EJ Tel: 01722 555121/0/3 www.salisburycathedral.org.uk

SHEFFIELD CATHEDRAL Church Street, Sheffield S1 1HA Tel: 0114 275 3434 www.sheffield-cathedral.org.uk

SHEFFIELD RC CATHEDRAL Norfolk Street, Sheffield S1 2JB Tel: 0114 272 2522 www.stmariecathedral-sheffield.org

SHREWSBURY RC CATHEDRAL Cathedral House, 11 Belmont, Shrewsbury SY1 1TE Tel: 01743 362366

SOUTHWARK CATHEDRAL Montague Close, London SE1 9DA Tel: 020 7367 6700 www.dswark.org

SOUTHWARK RC CATHEDRAL Cathedral House, Westminster Bridge Road, London SE1 7HY Tel: 020 7928 5256 www.southwark-rc-cathedral.org.uk

SOUTHWELL MINSTER The Minster Office, Bishops Drive, Southwell, Nottinghamshire NG25 0JP Tel: 01636 812649 www.southwellminster.org.uk

TRURO CATHEDRAL Cathedral Office, 14 St Mary's Street, Truro TR1 2AF Tel: 01872 276782 www.trurocathedral.org.uk

WAKEFIELD CATHEDRAL Northgate, Wakefield WF1 1HG Tel: 01924 373923 www.wakefield-cathedral.org.uk

WELLS CATHEDRAL Cathedral Offices, Chain Gate, Cathedral Green, Wells, Somerset BA5 2UE Tel: 01749 674483 www.wellscathedral.org.uk

WESTMINSTER ABBEY The Chapter Office, 20 Dean's Yard, Westminster Abbey, London SW1P 3PA Tel: 020 7222 5152 www.westminster-abbey.org

WESTMINSTER RC CATHEDRAL Cathedral Clergy House, 42 Francis Street, London SW1P 1QW Tel: 020 7798 9055/6 www.westminstercathedral.org.uk

WINCHESTER CATHEDRAL Cathedral Office, 1 The Close, Winchester, Hampshire SO23 9LS Tel: 01962 857200 www.winchester-cathedral.org.uk

WORCESTER CATHEDRAL Chapter Office, 10A College Green, Worcester WR1 2LH Tel: 01905 28854/21004 www.cofe-worcester.org.uk/cathedral/

YORK MINSTER Visitors Department, St Williams College, 4-5 College Street, York Y01 7JF Tel: 01904 557216 www.yorkminster.org

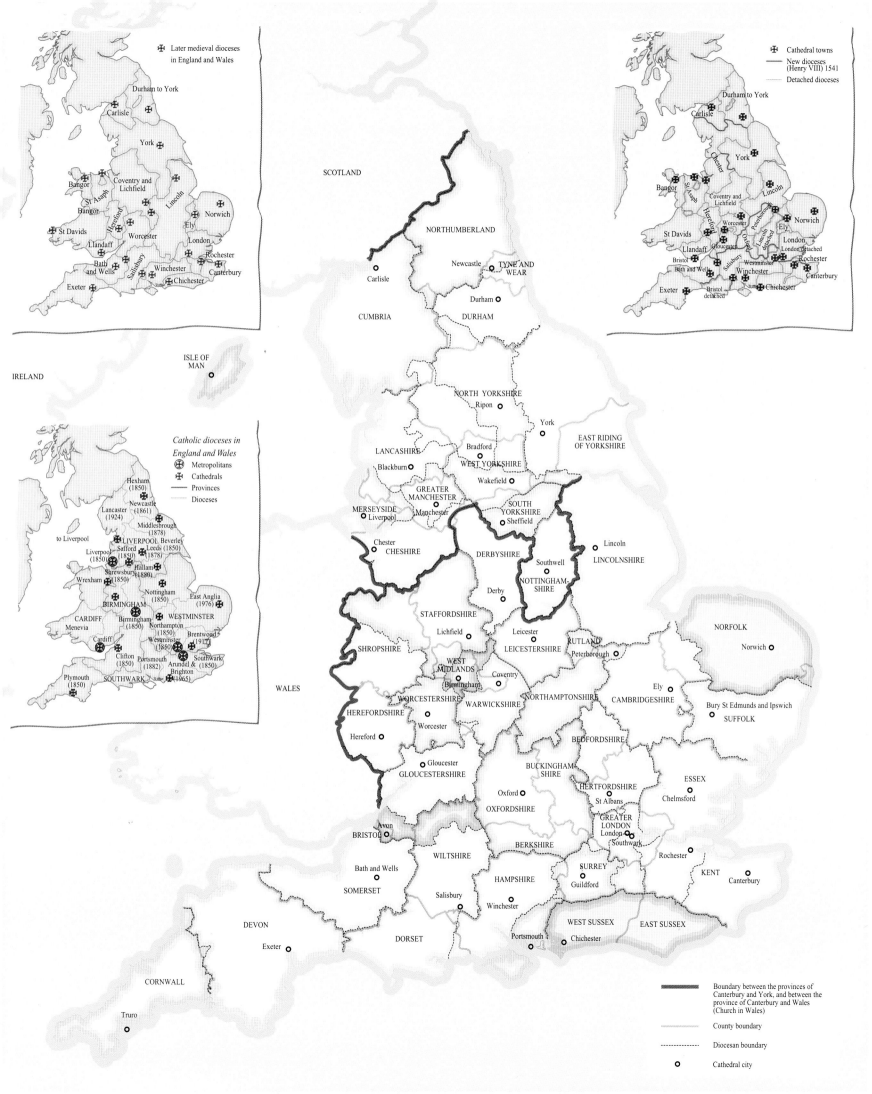

Inset top-left:

Later medieval dioceses in England and Wales ✠

Durham to York
Carlisle ✠
York ✠
Bangor ✠
Coventry and Lichfield ✠
St Asaph
Bangor
Hereford ✠
Lincoln ✠
Norwich ✠
St Davids ✠
Ely ✠
Llandaff ✠
Worcester ✠
London ✠
Bath and Wells ✠
Salisbury ✠
Winchester ✠
Rochester ✠
Canterbury ✠
Exeter ✠
Chichester ✠

Inset top-right:

✠ Cathedral towns
— New dioceses (Henry VIII) 1541
···· Detached dioceses

Durham to York
Carlisle ✠
Chester ✠
York ✠
Bangor ✠
St Asaph
Lincoln ✠
Coventry and Lichfield ✠
Peterborough ✠
Norwich ✠
St Davids ✠
Hereford ✠
Worcester ✠
Ely ✠
Gloucester ✠
Oxford ✠
Lincoln detached
London ✠
Bristol ✠
Salisbury ✠
Westminster ✠
London detached
Bath and Wells ✠
Winchester ✠
Rochester ✠
Exeter ✠
Bristol detached
Chichester ✠
Canterbury ✠

Inset lower-left:

Catholic dioceses in England and Wales
✠ Metropolitans
✠ Cathedrals
— Provinces
···· Dioceses

Hexham (1850)
Lancaster (1924)
Newcastle (1861)
Middlesbrough (1878)
to Liverpool
LIVERPOOL
Beverley
Liverpool (1850)
Salford (1850)
Leeds (1850)
Shrewsbury (1850)
Hallam (1980)
Wrexham
Nottingham (1850)
East Anglia (1976)
BIRMINGHAM
CARDIFF
Menevia
Birmingham (1850)
Northampton (1850)
WESTMINSTER
Brentwood (1917)
Westminster (1850)
Cardiff (1850)
Clifton (1850)
Portsmouth (1882)
Southwark (1850)
Arundel & Brighton (1965)
Plymouth (1850)
SOUTHWARK

Main map labels:

SCOTLAND
IRELAND
ISLE OF MAN

NORTHUMBERLAND
Newcastle
TYNE AND WEAR
Carlisle
CUMBRIA
DURHAM
Durham
NORTH YORKSHIRE
Ripon
York
EAST RIDING OF YORKSHIRE
LANCASHIRE
Bradford
WEST YORKSHIRE
Blackburn
Wakefield
GREATER MANCHESTER
MERSEYSIDE
Liverpool
Manchester
SOUTH YORKSHIRE
Sheffield
Chester
CHESHIRE
DERBYSHIRE
Southwell
Lincoln
LINCOLNSHIRE
Derby
NOTTINGHAM-SHIRE
STAFFORDSHIRE
Lichfield
Leicester
LEICESTERSHIRE
RUTLAND
Peterborough
NORFOLK
Norwich
SHROPSHIRE
WEST MIDLANDS
Birmingham
Coventry
NORTHAMPTONSHIRE
Ely
CAMBRIDGESHIRE
Bury St Edmunds and Ipswich
SUFFOLK
WALES
WORCESTERSHIRE
Worcester
WARWICKSHIRE
BEDFORDSHIRE
HEREFORDSHIRE
Hereford
Gloucester
GLOUCESTERSHIRE
BUCKINGHAM-SHIRE
Oxford
HERTFORDSHIRE
St Albans
Chelmsford
ESSEX
OXFORDSHIRE
GREATER LONDON
London
Southwark
Rochester
Avon
BRISTOL
BERKSHIRE
SURREY
Guildford
KENT
Canterbury
WILTSHIRE
HAMPSHIRE
Bath and Wells
Salisbury
Winchester
SURREY
SOMERSET
DEVON
DORSET
Portsmouth
Chichester
WEST SUSSEX
EAST SUSSEX
Exeter
CORNWALL
Truro

Main legend (bottom right):

━━ Boundary between the provinces of Canterbury and York, and between the province of Canterbury and Wales (Church in Wales)

░░ County boundary

···· Diocesan boundary

○ Cathedral city

INDEX

Page numbers in **bold** refer to main
references and illustrations
Page numbers in *italics* refer to captions